# Scats
## and
# Tracks
### of the
## Great Lakes

T0002589

# Scats
## and
# Tracks
## of the
## Great Lakes

*A Field Guide to the Signs of Seventy Wildlife Species*

Second Edition

James C. Halfpenny, PhD

Illustrated by Todd Telander

GUILFORD, CONNECTICUT
HELENA, MONTANA

An imprint of Rowman & Littlefield

Falcon, FalconGuides, and Outfit Your Mind are registered trademarks of
Rowman & Littlefield.

Distributed by NATIONAL BOOK NETWORK

Copyright © 2015 by Rowman & Littlefield

A previous edition of this book was published by Globe Pequot Press in 2006.

Illustrations by Todd Telander

*All rights reserved.* No part of this book may be reproduced in any form or by
any electronic or mechanical means, including information storage and retrieval
systems, without written permission from the publisher, except by a reviewer who
may quote passages in a review.

British Library Cataloguing-in-Publication Information Available

**Library of Congress Cataloging-in-Publication Data**

Halfpenny, James C.

  Scats and tracks of the Great Lakes : a field guide to the signs of 70 wildlife
species / James C. Halfpenny, PhD; illustrated by Todd Telander. — Second
edition.

     pages cm

  Includes bibliographical references and index.

  ISBN 978-1-4930-0992-3 (pbk.) — ISBN 978-1-4930-1515-3 (e-book)  1.
Animal tracks—Great Lakes Region (North America)  2.  Tracking and trailing—
Great Lakes Region (North America)  3.  Animal droppings—Great Lakes
Region (North America)  I. Title.

  QL768.H3543 2015

  596.0977—dc23

                                    2015018280

⊗™  The paper used in this publication meets the minimum requirements of
American National Standard for Information Sciences—Permanence of Paper for
Printed Library Materials, ANSI/NISO Z39.48-1992.

The authors and Rowman & Littlefield assume no liability for accidents happening to, or injuries sustained by, readers who engage in the activities described in this book.

## CAUTION

Outdoor recreational activities are by their very nature potentially hazardous. All participants in such activities must assume responsibility for their own actions and safety. The information contained in this guidebook cannot replace sound judgment and good decision-making skills, which help reduce exposure, nor does the scope of this book allow for the disclosure of all the potential hazards and risks involved in such activities. Learn as much as possible about the outdoor recreational activities in which you participate, prepare for the unexpected, and be cautious. The reward will be a safer and more enjoyable experience.

*To the late Pam Troxell for the miles we covered,
for the tracks we followed, for all she did to
share nature and wolves with everyone, and for
her constant smile! Travel softly, my friend!*

*To Beth Tiller and the late Dave Tiller for starting
my tracking in the Great Lakes region, for the
tracks we followed, and for their steadfast support
of the science of tracking! Travel softly my friends!*

*To Diann, my alpha partner, ursophile, and
tracking friend, for all her loving support and help!*
*JH*

# Contents

# Acknowledgments

First and foremost, I wish to thank all my students for their years of questions and help, but most of all for the time we've shared tracking and studying in the field. I also wish to thank Jim Bruchac (Ndakinna, New York) for the miles we shared tracking, Lee Fitzhugh, Larry Marlow, Sue Morse (Keeping Track, Jericho, Vermont) for her help with lynx track information, Murie Museum, Teton Science School, and Terry McEneany (Yellowstone National Park) for his help with bird tracks.

My heartfelt thanks to Tim Bennett, Sara Boles, Alice Droske, June Emerson, Bob Evans, Mark Gleason, Jim Hammill, John Heusinkveld, Dorothy Mcleer, Patrick Nagi, John Olson, Rolf Peterson, Beth Rogers, Ron Schultz, Tim Schaub, Jim Scott, Dave Stiller, Eric Trott, Pam Troxell, Nancy Warren, Al Warren, and Adrian Wydeven for the great times we have shared tracking in the Great Lakes area.

The following organizations have been instrumental in hosting tracking programs in the Great Lakes region: Bay Cliff Health Center, Isle Royale Institute, Ottawa National Forest, Ralph A. McMullan Center, See-North, Sigurd Olson Environmental Institute Northland College, Timberwolf Alliance, University of Michigan Pelson Field Station, University of Wisconsin at Steven's Point Treehaven Field Station, and Wisconsin Department of Natural Resources.

## Introduction

By the late 1970s, the era of watchable wildlife had arrived in the United States. Baby boomers wanted to turn to and experience the outdoors. Television brought wildlife closer than ever. Birding thrived. Today, more than ever, millions of people want to watch wild animals. Wildlife is not always easy to find and observe, though. Finding animal tracks and signs is an exciting alternative to seeing the animals themselves. Trackable wildlife adds another dimension to the outdoor experience. Todd and I wish to share that dimension—the joy of reading stories written in the soil and snow.

Upwards of ten books on tracking were written in the United States during each decade of the twentieth century, and that trend continues in the twenty-first century. Most of these books are general, covering the United States or all of North America. In *Scats and Tracks of the Great Lakes*, we focus on one biogeographic region, with details about the region's most common or characteristic species of mammals, birds, reptiles, and amphibians. (We have included a few rare species because of their particular interest or significance in a region.) We've intentionally limited the number of species covered in order to keep the information manageable. This guide is small, allowing you to carry it in a pack or pocket and use it frequently.

As your knowledge and interest in tracking grows, you may want to find additional information and help. Key references are listed in Selected Reading. For a more detailed investigation of tracking, I recommend my book *A Field Guide to Mammal Tracking in North America* (1986), and titles by Mark Elbroch, Louis Liebenberg, Jim Lowery, David Moskowitz, Olaus Murie, L. R. Forrest, and Paul Rezendes.

Our organization provides interactive access to expand your tracking background A Naturalist's World (ANW) is an ecologically oriented company dedicated to providing educational programs and materials that reflect the natural history of North America. Diann Thompson and I run the daily business, teach classes, and lead programs. Our on-site classes provide hands-on experience and in-depth information about animals, their tracks, and the ecology of their environments. In addition to tracking classes, our field programs cover bears, wolves, winter ecology, the northern lights, and alpine ecology. ANW also provides books, videos, slide shows, and computer programs for self-study and as teaching and field aids. Class schedules, product information, and information about ANW can be obtained from PO Box 989, Gardiner, MT 59030; (406) 848-9458; www.tracknature.com. For forensic tracking help, go to our subsidiary, TrackSceneInvestigations.com.

Keep on tracking!

—*James C. Halfpenny*

## About Tracking

Tracking is for everyone, beginner and expert, young and old. The fun of nature's challenge is solving the mystery written in the trail. Prepare yourself by learning the background and basics of tracking before exercising your skills in the field.

### Field Notes and Preserving Tracks

To the natural history detective, the track and trail are things of great beauty and significance. They tell part of the story of an animal's life. Tracks and trails deserve to be preserved, both to increase your knowledge and as a record you can share with others. Preservation is commonly made in the form of written notes, casts, or photographs.

Perhaps the most important item in the naturalist's tool kit is the field notebook. Field notes can jog the memory and facilitate better retention of knowledge. The notes can be analyzed later and can be preserved as records of chance encounters. Writing good field notes is an art form and a science in itself. Field notes are a source of pride when shown to others and may gain recognition for recording rare and unusual events. And need we mention how quickly memories, especially for details, fade when not preserved?

While great and complex systems have been designed for complete and accurate records, there are really but three requirements for the tracker: ruler, paper, and pen. With these, every trail becomes a record for later analysis and sharing. We cannot emphasize enough the importance of enhancing your tracking experience by keeping notes to which you can later refer!

A simple 3 × 5-inch notebook and a 6-inch ruler are adequate to get started. Use a pencil or a pen with ink that won't run if your notes get wet. To facilitate taking notes, ANW produces a waterproof notebook that contains information about footprint groups, gaits, and how to track and data sheets for recording information. English and metric rulers are imprinted on the back cover. See the introduction for ANW contact information.

Tracks may also be preserved by photographing and making casts. Good photographs can be made by any modern camera that can take a good close-up. When taking pictures, try to fill the viewfinder with the footprint; get as close as possible. Always include a ruler or some other object in the photo to provide a sense of scale. Avoid using hats, gloves, hands, or objects without a straight edge; round edges do not lend themselves to making accurate measurements from a photo. To avoid distortion, take the photograph from directly above the track, shooting straight down. Also, step back and take photographs of the trail to show the footprints that were photographed close-up.

Plaster casts are the old standby for preserving tracks. We suggest a casting kit that includes a 1-gallon (4-liter) plastic jar with a screw lid for carrying dry plaster, a narrow spatula, a plastic mixing cup such as those sold for medium-size drinks, paper for wrapping and transporting the finished cast, and a plastic sack for cleanup. A bottle of water may be needed if water is not available on-site. Two pounds of plaster will make at least four coyote-size track casts.

Purchase plaster from a lumberyard or hardware store, where prices will be more reasonable than at a drugstore or hobby shop. Almost any plaster will work, including plaster of paris, Hydrocal, Ultracal, or Hydrostone. Avoid getting plaster labeled Polyplaster or plaster for wallboard or patching compound, however. These plasters are formulated to be slightly flexible on walls and do not get hard enough for casts.

Two factors are critical to prevent casts from breaking: thickness and density. In the field, thickness is assured by building a wall around the track to contain the plaster.

Natural objects such as twigs, stones, and dirt may be used to make a retaining wall 0.25–0.5 inch (0.6–1.3 cm) above the track. Alternatively, walls in the form of plastic strips cut from milk cartons or other plastic containers may be taken to the field. Proper density is assured by mixing two parts of plaster to one part of water by volume (read instructions on plaster container) to create a mixture similar in consistency to thick pancake batter or a milkshake.

Place your spatula close to the track and pour onto the spatula to break the fall of the plaster into the footprint. Working quickly, so the plaster does not set and become too thick, gently pour the plaster first into the fine detailed areas of the footprint and then the rest of the print. Finally, pour the plaster to an appropriate depth inside the retaining wall to keep the cast from breaking. Vibrating the spatula up and down across the top of the plaster will cause air bubbles to rise and the plaster to settle evenly, creating a smooth back for the cast.

Allow the plaster to dry for 30 minutes, or as long as is recommended on the plaster package. Gently pick up the plaster by digging your fingers under opposite sides of the cast, and turn the cast over onto one hand. Now wash off the dirt by rubbing the cast with your fingertips under the flowing water of a stream or a hose. Do not wash the cast in a sink as plaster may clog the drain. Let the cast continue to cure for several days in a warm, dry environment. If you need to transport it, wrap the cast in paper. Never wrap the cast in plastic; trapped moisture may cause it to crumble.

While special techniques are needed for casts made in dust and snow, the above procedure will allow casting in many situations. Remember, carry a plastic garbage bag and always clean up your mess. No sign of your plaster should remain to reduce the experience of others who happen by later.

## Make Your Own Track Plates

Another method of preserving tracks is to use track plates. A track plate is a surface coated with a material that clings to the animal's feet and leaves a minimum outline print on a collection board. Soot and chalk make good recording materials. (My book *Track Plates for Mammals: A How-to Manual and Aid to Footprint Identification* explains the many types and methods of making track plates.)

Make a low-cost, simple track plate box by cutting one end out of a small cardboard box. Fix a piece of clear contact paper, sticky side down, to the bottom of the box near the opening. Fix a second piece, sticky side up, to the back half using rings of tape. Place bait at the closed end of the box. Peanut butter is good bait for many animals.

To record the tracks, make a thin paste of carpenter's chalk (available at hardware stores) mixed with rubbing alcohol and spread it onto the contact paper at the open end. As the alcohol evaporates, the chalk sticks to the paper and the powder will not blow away. The box is now ready.

When the animal walks across the chalk, the powder sticks to its feet. When the animal then steps on the sticky paper, great prints are recorded. Place a piece of blank paper onto the sticky paper and then remove it. The clear contact paper will show the footprints, which can then be copied.

## Scats and Bird Pellets

Scats and bird pellets (also called cough pellets or castings) are often helpful for identifying an animal or completing the story that's written in the trail. Scats and pellets help identify not only what the animal was eating but also who the animal was. However, it should be noted that scats and pellets won't help you identify an animal with as much certainty as identification by tracks. Many animals make similar scats and pellets that are difficult to tell apart.

The scats of many carnivores are very similar, especially when the diet is mostly meat. Size alone does not provide a definitive answer because of the wide range of diameters produced within a species and even by a single member of a species. For example, foxes produce scats ranging in size from 0.3 to 0.8 inch (0.8–2 cm), coyotes produce scats 0.5-1.3 inches (1.3–3.3 cm), wolves produce scats 0.5–1.5 inches (1.3–3.8 cm), and we all know how our own scat varies in size and shape. When judging size, consider both the total quantity of scat and the size of individual pieces. Moist food produces slimmer scats, while fibrous diets produce wider scats.

Given these cautions, scat shapes can be used to identify general groups of animals (see page xx). Spherical shapes flattened top to bottom are deposited by members of the rabbit order. Elongate spheres are deposited by rodents and shrews, and at larger sizes by deer and their relatives. Long, thick cords are deposited by dogs, bears, and raccoons. Dog scats typically have tapered ends, while those from bears and raccoons are blunt. Cats also produce thick cords with blunt ends, but they tend to be constricted or even broken into short segments. Cords that loop back on themselves are produced by members of the weasel family. Birds, in general, produce long, thin cords or shapeless, semiliquid excretions. Reptiles and amphibians may produce small elongate spheres or long, thin cords. White, nitrogenous urine deposits, found on the scats of birds, reptiles, and amphibians, separate them from mammal scats.

Scats may be confused with cough pellets. Many bird groups, including owls, raptors, crows, ravens, jays, magpies, gulls, herons, storks, flycatchers, and kingfishers, produce cough pellets in addition to scats. Birds pass digestive juices through what they have eaten to remove the nutrients. Hair, bones, beaks, claws, and other non-digestible parts accumulate in the gizzard (anterior portion of stomach), are compressed, and are coughed up as pellets. Food remnants in the pellet are easy to identify and tell much about the bird's feeding habits and even the habitats it frequents.

**cough pellet**

Pellets are grayish and are spherical or long and tapered at both ends. When fresh, they are covered by mucus and appear dark black. Pellets are found mainly at roosting sites and nests, and occasionally at feeding areas. They are deposited singly, but many may accumulate beneath a tree where a bird is roosting, nesting, or perching. Nitrogenous scat deposits on the ground or twigs may help verify an object as a pellet.

The diameter of the bird's throat determines the maximum diameter of the pellet. In general, large birds produce larger pellets. Shape and diameter allow one to distinguish to some degree between species.

Birds generally produce two pellets per day and regurgitate just before taking flight. The time of day when feeding occurred may affect the sample of food items. For example, owls tend to feed on mammals that come out only at night, while hawks feed on animals that are out during the daylight hours.

### Anatomy and Footprint Nomenclature

The feet of mammals, birds, reptiles, and amphibians are anatomically complex, and that complexity shows in their footprints. Knowing something of the anatomy of their feet will aid in footprint identification and interpreting trails.

The toes of all animals are numbered from the inside of the foot out (the inside of the foot being the side closest to the animal). Therefore, in humans and other mammals, the thumb or big toe (if present) is number 1 and the little

## Shapes of Scats

**Spheres**
Rabbits and their
relatives

rabbit

**Spheres, elongate**
Rodents, shrews,
deer, and their
relatives

woodrat

shrew

elk

**Cords, long
and thick**
Wolves, coyotes,
bears, raccoons,
and their relatives

coyote

bear

raccoon

**Cords, thick and
often constricted**
Mountain lions and their
relatives

mountain lion

**Cords, often folded**
Weasels and their relatives

mink

**Cords, long and thin,
often with
nitrogenous deposits**
Birds, reptiles, and amphibians

Canada goose

lizard

finger or little toe is number 5. In birds, toe 1 (if present) points backward.

Over evolutionary time, toes of animals have become reduced in size or have disappeared altogether. In cats and dogs, toe 1 is absent or reduced to a small toe called a dewclaw. In deer, elk, sheep, and similar mammals, toe 1 is absent and toes 2 and 5 are reduced and form dewclaws. Toes 3 and 4, known as clouts, form the cloven hoof. In pronghorn antelope, toes 1, 2, and 5 are absent. In birds, toe 5 is absent; toe 1 is often reduced and occasionally absent. In the amphibians covered here, toe 1 has been lost from the front foot.

## Track Measurements

To more accurately determine the animal's foot size from its tracks, mountain lion researchers Dave Fjelline and Terri Mansfield (1989) developed a process now called the "minimum outline method" of measuring tracks.

Place your hand on a hard surface, a table for instance. Note the contact area of your hand with that surface. If your hand went no deeper into that surface, your handprint would have only one size, the minimum outline. If your hand were to sink deeper into the surface, as it would if the surface were, say, mud, it would create a series of variable outlines, each larger than the one before, as the mud flowed around the curved surface of your hand. All footprints have a minimum outline, but only prints that sink a surface have variable outlines.

Note that while the variable outline of a footprint may only be several millimeters larger than the minimum outline, those few millimeters have a large visual effect. The human eye sees area, and area increases with the square of a linear measurement. In short, a few millimeters of width add a lot of area to a footprint.

The minimum outline size does not change for different surfaces, and therefore it provides a standard for comparison between surfaces. And though one animal may leave many sizes of footprints depending on surface, slope, and speed, there is only one minimum outline for every footprint an animal might leave. The minimum outline measurement is the only constant and consistent size in tracking.

To measure the minimum outline, study the bottom of a print. The *break point* where the rounded pad turns upward is the edge of the minimum outline. Use this edge to measure tracks.

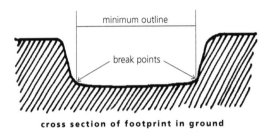

**cross section of footprint in ground**

Assigning the break point is a subjective judgment, and no two people will always mark it at exactly the same point. However, testing has shown that an individual tracker using the minimum outline method can reduce personal variation in measurement and that groups of trackers using this method will also become more consistent in their measurement of tracks. Remember the computer rule GIGO: garbage in, garbage out. You cannot get quality measurements from a bad track. Quality measurements are the tracker's goal, and using minimum outline methods greatly reduce overexaggeration and variance in measurement.

All measurements in this guide are minimum outline measurements.

The measurements in *Scats and Tracks of the Great Lakes* are mostly averages gathered from years of tracking.

Averages include only animals judged to be adult. However, it is important to remember the great size variation among animals. Every animal was small once in its life, and some never get big. Males are often substantially larger than females. Regional variations in mammal sizes also occur. For example, coyotes are smaller in the southwestern United States and larger in the northeastern part of the country. Their tracks vary accordingly. Therefore, a track in the field may be considerably larger or smaller than the measurements provided here. Use track measurements only as a rough guideline, not as an absolute rule.

## Gaits and Trails

Coordinated muscle movements result in the various gaits used by animals. In the simplest form, when moving on two legs (bipedal movement) an organism can *walk*, *run*, and *hop*. When moving on four legs (quadrupedal movement) an organism can *walk*, *trot*, *lope*, *gallop*, *bound*, and *pronk* (also called *stot*). Though other gaits exist, we will confine our discussion to these basic gaits. Each gait leaves a characteristic pattern that may be modified by changes in speed and body angle. The combination of footprints is called the *trail*. The bipedal walk and run and the quadrupedal walk and trot result in gaits that are *symmetrical*. The right side of the trail is a mirror image of the left side. The trail patterns for these gaits are the same alternating right-left pattern and differ only by the stride being longer in the run and trot than it is in the walk. In

walk    trot

the run and trot, the straddle—the distance from the right edge of the rightmost pad (see pages xxvi and xxxii) to the left edge of the leftmost pad—also tends to be narrower than it is in the walk.

Quadrupedal movement also results in gaits that are *asymmetrical* (the right half of the trail is not always a mirror image of the left), including lope, gallop, bound, hop, and pronk. These gaits produce patterns that include all four footprints (two fronts, two hinds, two rights, and two lefts) in a group separated from the next group by a space where no footprints appear.

In *gallops*, the feet, front and rear, that move first (or *lead*) will determine whether the gallop will form a Z-shape or C-shaped pattern. When the front and hind feet on the same side lead, the pattern takes on a Z shape. A right-front lead with a left-hind lead, or vice versa, results in a C-shaped pattern. Thus, there are four possible gallop patterns.

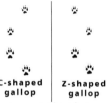

C-shaped gallop   Z-shaped gallop

large print-front feet
small print-rear feet

*Bounds* (also known as hops and jumps) are characterized by the synchronization of the hind feet; both strike the ground at the same time, side by side. The front feet strike the ground at a different time than the hind feet. In a full bound, the front feet are synchronized and strike the ground side by side at the same time. In a half bound, only the hind feet are synchronized and the front feet hit the ground staggered. Animals that mostly use full bounds, also called hops, live in trees (tree squirrels), whereas those that mostly use half bounds live on the ground (ground squirrels and rabbits). Birds (mostly songbirds) that use a

full bound   half bound

full bound live in trees; ground birds (mostly shorebirds) use a half bound.

In a *pronk* (also called a *stot*), all four feet strike the ground at the same time, with the front feet side by side and forward of the hind feet, which are also side by side. This gait is often used by deer to gain height and increase time in the air to look around.

**pronk**

To increase peripheral vision, non-primate mammals have eyes placed toward the sides of their heads, not flat on their face like humans. By turning sideways, a prey species can see what is pursuing it and where it needs to go to escape. The predator, by turning sideways, can see what it is chasing and where the rest of the predator pack is.

Consequently, quadrupedal mammals have evolved to use all gaits while their body is turned to the side. These *side gaits* result when the animal's heavy head deviates from the line of travel and the body turns sideways. First, the front feet respond by moving toward the side of the trail where the head is. Then, as the head turns more, the hind feet move to the side away from the head. The greater the head movement, the greater the angle of the side gait. Common examples are the side trot and side gallop often used by canids. These are often called a dog trot or dog gallop.

**slow side trot**  **side gallop**

An animal's size is also reflected in its gait patterns. When a mammal is walking with its normal gait, for example, the stride is 1 to 1.25 times longer than the distance from the hip to the shoulder joint. Using this crude relationship, body size can be judged from a walking stride. A

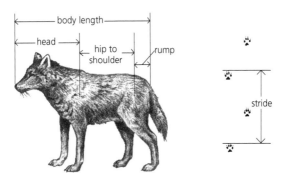

**Estimating mammal length from stride**

20-inch stride indicates a hip-to-shoulder length of 20 inches. Add to the hip-to-shoulder distance an estimate for the head length beyond the shoulder joint and an estimate of the rump length beyond the hip joint to get a total estimate of animal body length.

Speed also modifies gait patterns in trails. There are three rules governing how pattern changes as speed changes:

1. As speed increases, the hind foot lands farther forward than the front footprint on the same side. Conversely, as speed decreases, the hind foot lands farther back in relation to the front footprint.
2. As speed increases, stride increases.
3. As speed increases, straddle usually decreases.

Speed changes are easily observed in quadrupedal walk and trot trail patterns. As speed increases, the hind footprint registers in front of the front print. This faster version of a walk is called an *amble*. The faster version of a

walk
(slower)

amble
(faster)

trot doesn't have a name. When the animal slows to the point that the hind feet are registering behind the front prints, the animal may be stalking something. Trots are separated from walks by having a stride two or more times greater than the estimated hip-to-shoulder distance of an animal.

A slow version of the gallop is also recognizable. When a gallop slows to the point that one or more hind feet register behind the leading edge of the frontmost footprint in a group pattern, the gait is called a *lope*. The lope gait is still a gallop; it's just a slow gallop.

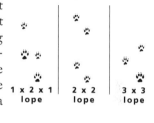

## Trail Measurements

The terms *stride*, *group*, *intergroup*, and *straddle* describe the size of an animal trail. The *stride* is measured from the point where a foot touches the ground surface to where the same point of the same foot next touches the surface, and consists of one group and one intergroup measurement. The *group* consists of all four footprints (two fronts, two hinds, two lefts, two rights), while the *intergroup* is the distance between groups. Gait patterns take their name from the configuration of the group. The stride provides an indication of size in a walking animal and an indication of relative speed for other gaits (see pages xxvi and above).

The *straddle* indicates the width of the trail and is measured from the outside rightmost pad of the outside right footprint of a group to the outside leftmost pad footprint of the same group. The outside edges of the trail are used because for many carnivore species the inside of footprints overlap. The outside straddle of a walking animal provides an estimate of body size.

# Glossary of Terms

**amble:** A fast walk in which the hind footprint registers anterior to the front footprint. See illustration on page xxvi.

**asymmetrical:** Not symmetrical; that is, one side is not a mirror image of the opposite side.

**bound:** A gait in which both hind feet strike the ground at the same time, side by side. If the front feet also land side by side, the motion is said to be a *full bound*. A *half bound* occurs when one front foot strikes the ground in front of the other. See illustration on page xxiv.

**clout:** Term used to refer to toe 3 or toe 4 of the hoof. See illustration on page xxxiii.

**convergent toes:** Toes 2 and 4 of ducks, geese, and swans, which bend toward the *foot axis*, especially at the tips. Compare to *divergent toes*.

**cord:** See *scat shape*.

**cough pellet:** Remnants of bones and hair coughed up by many bird species after feeding on prey.

**dewclaw:** Toe that over evolutionary time has become reduced in size and raised on the leg, away from the other toes. For example, toe 1 in dogs and toes 2 and 5 in deer.

**diagnostic:** Providing certain identification of an animal or its sign.

**digit:** One of the toes of an animal.

**digital pad:** See *pad*.

**digitigrade:** Walking on the tips of the toes. Dogs and cats, for example, are digitigrade. Tracks left by digitigrade animals rarely show a *sole*. Compare to *plantigrade*.

**distal webbing:** See *webbing*.

**divergent toes:** Toes that are straight or turn out from the *foot axis* at the tips, specifically toes 2 and 4 of sea gulls. Compare to *convergent toes*.

**foot axis:** Imaginary line down the center of the foot. It runs between toes 3 and 4 in deer and their relatives, and down toe 3 of other mammals. In birds, the foot axis also runs down toe 3.

**fringe:** Webbing attached to a single toe. May have a smooth edge, known as a *simple fringe* or *simple lobe*, or it may be wavy, in which case it is said to have *indented lobes*.

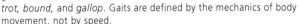
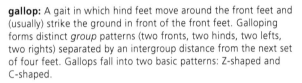

**full bound:** See *bound*.

**gait:** Term for the type(s) of movement an animal uses when moving. Examples of gaits include *walk, amble, trot, bound,* and *gallop*. Gaits are defined by the mechanics of body movement, not by speed.

**gallop:** A gait in which hind feet move around the front feet and (usually) strike the ground in front of the front feet. Galloping forms distinct *group* patterns (two fronts, two hinds, two lefts, two rights) separated by an intergroup distance from the next set of four feet. Gallops fall into two basic patterns: Z-shaped and C-shaped.

**group:** A subunit of a *stride* including four footprints (two fronts and two hinds, and two lefts and two rights). The measure of the group plus the intergroup equals the measure of the stride.

**half bound:** See *bound*.

**heel:** Portion of foot or track to the rear of digital and interdigital pads. In mammals, may be covered with hair, naked (without hair), or have one or more proximal pads. In reptiles and amphibians, may be textured with *tubercles*.

**hop:** Synonymous with *bound*, often used in reference to gaits of rodents and rabbits.

**indented lobe:** See *fringe*.

**interdigital pad:** See *pad*.

**length:** Of a track, the distance from front of toe *pads* to back of the interdigital pads, measured parallel to the foot *axis*. In mammal tracks, does not include claws. In bird tracks, does not include toe 1, but includes claws if they are attached and indistinguishable from toe pad.

**line of travel:** Imaginary line on the ground over which the center of gravity of an animal passes.

**lobe:** See *fringe*.

**lope:** A slow *gallop* in which at least one hind foot registers behind a front foot in a group of four footprints. See illustration on page xxvii.

**mesial webbing:** See *webbing*.

**minimum outline:** See pages xxi–xxii for extended discussion.

**nipple-dimple:** See *scat shape*.

**outer toe angle:** In birds, the angle between toes 2 and 4. In perching birds, less than 90 degrees; in shorebirds, greater than 120 degrees.

**oval:** See *scat shape*.

**pad:** Hard, callus-like structure on the sole of an animal's foot. Each toe may have a digital pad. One or more interdigital pads are located directly to the rear of the toes, and one or more proximal pads may be located directly to the rear of the interdigital pads. In deer and their relatives, there is a single pad separated from the *wall* by the *subunguis*. In birds, a metatarsal pad may occur directly under the leg bone.

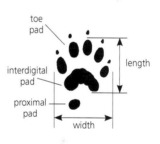

**plantigrade:** Walking on the soles of the foot. Raccoons, bears, and humans, for example, are plantigrade. The sole of the foot usually shows in the footprint. Compare to *digitigrade*.

**pronk:** A *gait* in which all four feet strike the ground simultaneously and directly below the body. The *group* pattern shows two front footprints ahead of the two hind prints. Also called a *stot*. See illustration on page xxv.

**proximal pad:** See *pad*.

**proximal webbing:** See *webbing*.

**rotary gallop:** A type of *gallop* that tends to form a C-shaped *group* pattern. See illustration on page xxiv.

**run:** A *gait* used when moving only on two legs. It differs from a *walk* in having a longer *stride*.

**scat shape:** *Cords* are long pieces of scat, typically four to ten times longer than the width. Ends may be blunt or tapered. *Ovals* are pieces of scat typically two to four times longer than wide and tapered at both ends. A *nipple-dimple* shaped scat pellet has a point at one end and a depression at the other. See chart on page xx.

**simple fringe, simple lobe:** See *fringe*.

**sole:** Bottom of an animal's foot. It may be covered with hair or naked, and may have one or more *pads* on it.

**stot:** See *pronk*.

**straddle:** The distance from the right edge of the rightmost pad to the leftmost edge of the leftmost pad in a *trail*. Measured at right angles to the *line of travel*.

stot

**stride:** The distance from the point where a foot touches the ground to the point where the same foot touches the ground again. Measured parallel to the *line of travel*. One stride is equal to a *group* plus an intergroup measurement.

**gallops**   **bounds**

intergroup

group

stride

intergroup

group

**subunguis:** The soft material under the nails of humans. In deer and their relatives, refers specifically to the soft material between the *pad* and *wall*.

**symmetrical:** Having two sides, one the mirror image of the other side.

**toe pad:** See *pad*.

**track:** Refers to an individual footprint. Some measurable characteristics include *length* and *width*.

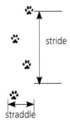

stride

straddle

**track pattern:** The gross visual image of the pattern of footprints on the ground. A repeating pattern of two prints separated from the next two is called two-by and written 2 × 2. Prints may also show patterns of 3 × 3, 4 × 4, and 1 × 2 × 1. These patterns are made during a *gallop* or a *bound*. A few of these patterns are illustrated on page xxiv.

**trail:** A series of footprints and associated sign that marks the passage of an animal. Some measurable characteristics include *stride* and *straddle*.

**transverse gallop:** A type of *gallop* that tends to form a Z-shaped group pattern. See illustration on page xxiv.

**trot:** A *gait* in which evenly spaced footprints alternate on right and left sides of the *line of travel*. Hind footprint registers on top of front. As speed increases, hind moves forward of front. Same patterns as a *walk*, but longer *stride*. May be done with body turned to side. See illustration on page xxiii.

**fast trot**

**tubercle:** Rough pinhead-size protuberance on the sole of the foot of a reptile or amphibian.

**unguis:** Hard material forming nails in humans, hoof walls in deer and their relatives, and claws in other mammals. Composed of hair pasted together by body glues.

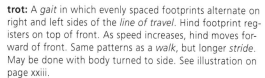

**walk:** A gait in which evenly spaced footprints alternate on right and left sides of the *line of travel*. Hind footprint registers on top of front. As speed increases, hind moves forward of front. See illustrations on pages xxiii and xxvi.

**wall:** Hard material around the edge of each clout of a hoof. Technically the *unguis,* which also forms human nails and animal claws.

**webbing:** Thin membrane stretched between toes of animals. The webbing may be near the tips of the toes

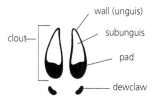

(*distal*), about midway to the toe tips (*mesial*), or attached at the base (*proximal*). A membrane attached to only one toe is called a *fringe*.

**width:** Of a *track,* the greatest distance from the right side of the pads of a foot to the left side, whether the greatest distance is across the toes or palm pads. Measured perpendicular to the *foot axis.* In bird tracks, includes claws if they are attached and indistinguishable from toe pad.

# How to Use *Scats and Tracks*

*Scats and Tracks of the Great Lakes* is designed for easy use in the field. The gray bars found on the edges of the pages of the track accounts will help you measure scat diameter and footprint size; each of these bars is keyed to the average size of the sign in question. A ruler is provided on the back cover. Below, we provide the background knowledge that every tracker should be familiar with before going to the field or using this book. Please take some time to study this material.

## Illustrations
Illustrator Todd Telander applied his great ability to our collections of plaster casts, photographs, and slides, drawing on our experience to produce the most up-to-date and accurate illustrations possible. These drawings are made from the best specimens in a collection of thousands, represent the culmination of decades of tracking experience, and are far more accurate than the tracker usually finds in tracking books. The tracks you find on the ground may not have as much detail or be as clear, but it is better to have an excellent drawing to compare to an imperfect track than to have to compare a track to a drawing lacking critical details.

## How to Use the Track Accounts
The track accounts in this guide have been grouped by similar footprint characteristics. Each track account represents a single species or a group of species with similar track characteristics. Each account is presented across a two-page spread and is conveniently divided into sections as discussed below.

Each account shows both a common and a scientific name. Below that is a brief listing of visual characteristics used to identify an animal. These descriptions are general, and great variability of pattern can exist among animals in the field. We recommend consulting appropriate field identification guides.

**Track:** A concise description of key points of footprints, to be used for identification. The accompanying track illustrations are not at actual size, but, unless otherwise noted, average length of the footprint is shown as a bar on the right side of the right-hand page. Average width is shown as a bar on the bottom of the right-hand page. In the field, place the appropriate measurement bar next to the track to compare size. To take a numerical measurement, use the ruler printed on the back cover of the book.

The tracks illustrated are all from right feet, except in the entries for birds, where both feet are pictured. Numerical measurements are given in the form *length × width*. Note that measurements of mammal tracks do not include claws, that measurements of bird tracks include claws but do not include toe 1, and that measurements generally do not include parts of the foot that often do not register in a given species' track (e.g., heels in the hind feet of some rodent species).

**Trail:** The average size of the stride of the most commonly used gait or gaits is given. Other common or characteristic gaits, if any, are discussed. See *track pattern* in the Glossary of Terms on page xxxiii. For more information on gaits in tracking, see *A Field Guide to Mammal Tracking in North America* by Jim Halfpenny. Gaits are displayed up the right side of the right-hand page. If the common gait is a walk or trot, however, it may not be illustrated, since all walking and trotting patterns consist of right-left alternating patterns.

**Scat:** A description of scat supplements the drawing. Average scat width is shown as a bar on the side of the left-hand page. In the field, place the appropriate measurement bar next to the scat to compare sizes. To take a numerical measurement, use the ruler printed on the back cover of the book. Numerical measurements of scat are given under the illustrations in the form *length* × *width*. In cases of small scat, only width is given; thus, a single measurement indicates diameter.

**Habitat:** To aid in locating and differentiating tracks, the animal's habitat preferences are listed. Some animals with large ranges, such as the beaver, are only found in specific habitats.

**Similar species:** Clues are provided to help differentiate an animal's tracks from similar tracks of other species. With these clues, identification should be possible.

**Other sign:** Other sign of animals, besides tracks and scat, are listed or illustrated to help with identification, and to provide more information on animal lives.

In addition, a distribution map is provided with each account. This gives a generalized picture of where in the Great Lakes region an animal may be found. Animals that require specific habitats will of course not be evenly distributed through the shown range.

To make the best use of this guide, carry it with you into the field. When you come across an unfamiliar track or trail, open the book to the appropriate track account and place the page alongside the track for immediate on-site comparison.

# Visual Key to Tracks

This simple key includes birds, reptiles, amphibians, and mammals. It is arranged by the number of toes that show in a good footprint, ranging from no toes to two toes to five toes. Those animals that show four toes in the front print and five toes in the hind are listed between four- and five-toed animals.

**Snakes** (pp. 20–21)
Series of side-to-side trail undulations.

**Deer and Relatives** (pp. 136–41)
Two toes form hard, cloven hoof. Dewclaws may show in deep print.

**Birds with Webbed Feet** (pp. 22–37, 54–57)
Three toes facing forward, often a fourth toe facing backward. Claws may be detached from toes. Webbing between two or more toes.

**Birds without Webbed Feet**
(pp. 38–53, 58–67)
Three toes facing forward, often a fourth toe facing backward. Claws may be detached from toes.

**Wolves, Dogs, and Relatives** (pp. 72–79)
Four toes in front and hind prints. Claws usually present and detached. Single anterior lobe on interdigital pad.

**Mountain Lions, Cats, and Relatives**
(pp. 80–85)
Four toes in front and hind prints. Claws usually absent. Double anterior lobe on interdigital pad.

### Rabbits and Relatives (pp. 104–9)

Four toes in front and hind footprint. An exceptionally clear print may show a fifth inner toe in the front footprint. Pads lacking, bottom of foot covered with hair. Long hopping heel in hind print.

### Rodents (pp. 110–35)

Most have four toes in front prints and five in hind. Beaver has five toes in front print. Front toes show a 1-2-1 grouping; hind show a 1-3-1 grouping. Long hopping heel in hind print.

### Salamanders (pp. 2–5)

Four toes in front print, five toes in hind. Trail wide, often with a tail drag.

### Frogs (pp. 8–13)

Four toes in front print, five toes in hind. Long, slender toes. Front print faces center of trail. Distal webbing in hind print.

### Toads (pp. 6–7)

Four toes in front print, five toes in hind. Front print faces center of trail. Mesial webbing in hind print. Tubercles may show on front and hind prints.

### Lizards (pp. 14–15)

Five toes in front and hind prints. Toes long and slender. Claws may be detached. Tail drag often present in trail.

### Turtles (pp. 16–19)

Five toes show in front and hind tracks. Front prints toe-in and hind prints may toe-out. Feet are relatively broad. Claws robust and often visible. Sometimes the claws are the only visible signs on hard ground.

### Opossum (pp. 68–69)

Five toes. Distinct hind print with an opposable (like human thumb) inside toe protruding sideways from other toes. Outside toe is slightly separated from middle three toes.

### Shrews (pp. 70–71)

Five slender toes present on front and hind feet. In clear prints, four interdigital and two proximal pads may be seen.

### Raccoon (pp. 88–89)

Five toes in front and hind prints. Toes often round or bulbous at ends. May have long, slender toes.

### Weasels and Relatives (pp. 90–103)

Five toes in front and hind prints, though the little toe (on inside of foot) may not show. Toes in a 1-3-1 grouping. Interdigital pad is chevron-shaped. Plantigrade hind foot.

### Black Bear (pp. 86–87)

Five toes in front and hind prints, though the little toe (on inside of foot) may not show. Toes evenly spaced. Plantigrade hind foot.

# Scats
### and
# Tracks
### of the

## Great Lakes

# Eastern Newt—Red Eft phase

*Notophthalmus viridescens*

Vienna sausage–size salamander, up to 4 inches (10 cm) long. Moist, smooth skin. Terrestrial form, called red eft, is bright orange red with red spots outlined in black. Tubercles on underside of foot.

**Track:** Four toes on front foot (often only three show); five toes on hind foot. The outline of the foot may not show, just toe prints. Even in a clear print, tubercles rarely show.

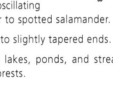

**Trail:** Walking stride is about 1 inch (2.5 cm). Trail has a wide straddle (0.67 inch/1.6 cm) relative to stride; may show oscillating belly and tail drag marks similar to spotted salamander.

**Scat:** Brown to black, rounded to slightly tapered ends.

**Habitat:** Quiet waters around lakes, ponds, and streams in grassland meadow areas and forests.

**scat**
0.2 x 0.1 in.
0.6 x 0.3 cm

SCAT WIDTH

**Similar species:** Differs from lizards by wider, oscillating tail drag (if present) and by having only four toes on front foot. Considerably smaller tracks and trail than most salamanders.

**Other sign:** Egg mass found in water along shore.

**front**
0.2 x 0.2 in.
0.5 x 0.5 cm

**hind**
0.2 x 0.1 in.
0.6 x 0.3 cm

**slow walk**

*FRONT TRACK LENGTH*

*FRONT TRACK WIDTH*

# Tiger Salamander
*Ambystoma tigrinum*

Hot dog–size
salamander, up
to 9 inches (23
cm) long. Moist,
smooth skin. Body
brown to black to
dark green, with yellow
spots or streaks. Tubercles on underside of foot.

**Track:** Four toes on front foot (often only three show), and five toes on hind foot. The outline of the foot may not show, just toe prints. Even in a clear print, tubercles rarely show.

**Trail:** Walking stride is about 3 inches (7.5 cm). Trail has a wide straddle relative to stride; may show oscillating belly and tail drag marks.

**scat**
0.3 x 0.2 in.
0.7 x 0.6 cm

**egg mass**

SCAT WIDTH

**Scat:** Soft, pea-size black masses with some hint of oval shape.

**Habitat:** Quiet waters around lakes, ponds, and streams in grassland meadow areas and forests.

**Similar species:** Differs from lizards by wider, oscillating tail drag and by having only four toes on front foot. Larger tracks and trail than newts.

**Other sign:** Eggs in egg masses are attached individually to underwater plant stems.

**front**
0.6 x 0.3 in.
1.5 x 0.8 cm

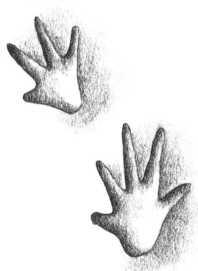

**hind**
0.8 x 0.6 in.
2 x 1.5 cm

**slow walk**

*FRONT TRACK LENGTH*

*FRONT TRACK WIDTH*

# American Toad
*Bufo americanus*

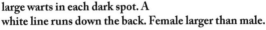

Baseball-size toad, up to 3.5 inches (9 cm) long. Body is plain brown to gray to reddish, with warts from yellow to red in dark brown or black spots. Only one or two large warts in each dark spot. A white line runs down the back. Female larger than male.

**Track:** Four toes on front foot and five on hind. Front feet face in. Two tubercles on heel of front foot. Three hind toes face in, one forward, and one out. Two tubercles may show on the heel of the hind foot and can be confused with toes. Webbing, found only on hind feet, extends at most halfway out to toe tips.

**Trail:** Hopping or full bound stride generally 5–7 inches (13–18 cm). Walking stride is about 2.5 inches (7.5 cm).

**Scat:** Dark brown to black. Long cord, up to five times longer than wide. Sometimes contains insect parts.

**scat**
0.9 x 0.2 in.
2.3 x 0.5 cm

**egg mass**

**toad imprint in mud**

**Habitat:** Lakes, ponds, beaver ponds, and wet mixed coniferous forest.

**Similar species:** Differs from frogs by presence of tubercles on front heels. Hind foot is narrower than frog. Walks and uses short hops more than the usually long-hopping frog.

**Other sign:** Long strings of egg masses on bottom of water source and floating among vegetation.

**walk**

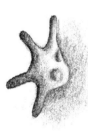

**front**
0.8 x 0.5 in.
2 x 1.3 cm

mesial web

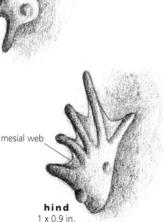

**hind**
1 x 0.9 in.
2.5 x 2.3 cm

**hop**

*FRONT TRACK LENGTH*

*FRONT TRACK WIDTH*

# Chorus Frog
*Pseudacris triseriata*

Silver dollar–size frog less than 1.5 inches (3.8 cm). Highly variable frog with body color from brown to green. Darker stripe pattern varies with subspecies.

**Track:** Four toes on front foot and five on hind. Front feet face in. Four hind toes face in, with one facing out. Proximal webbing on hind feet extending at most one-quarter of way out to toe tips.

**Trail:** Hopping stride about 10 inches (25 cm). Frogs may easily hop 3 feet (1 m) when in a hurry.

**scat**
0.5 x 0.1 in.
1.3 x 0.3 cm

**egg mass and tadpole**

SCAT WIDTH

**Scat:** Black, firm cord with slightly tapering ends.

**Habitat:** Shallow water with emergent vegetation, including pond and lake shores, marshes, and beaver ponds.

**Similar species:** Lacks the palm tubercles of the front feet of toad. Less webbing between toes. Hops more and longer distances. Smaller than leopard frog.

**Other sign:** Inconspicuous egg masses consisting of a few eggs in a packet attached to vegetation below water line.

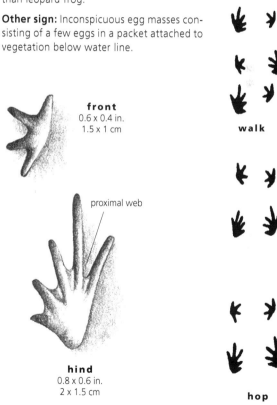

**front**
0.6 x 0.4 in.
1.5 x 1 cm

proximal web

**hind**
0.8 x 0.6 in.
2 x 1.5 cm

**walk**

**hop**

FRONT TRACK LENGTH

FRONT TRACK WIDTH

# Leopard Frog
*Rana pipiens*

Baseball-size frog, 3.5 inches (9 cm) long. Body light to dark brown or green, with dark spots. Spots have light borders. Head relatively long and pointed. White stripe on jaw. Often a light spot on eardrum.

**Track:** Four toes on front foot and five on hind. Front feet face in. Four hind toes face in, with one facing out. Webbing, found only on hind feet, is distal, extending most of the way out to toe tips. Toe 1 is thick on male because it serves as the nuptial pad for grasping female during mating.

**Trail:** Full bound or hopping stride is about 20 inches (50 cm). May easily hop 3 feet (1 m) when in a hurry. Occasionally walk.

**Scat:** Brown to black, with slightly tapered ends.

**scat**
1.5 x 0.4 in.
3.8 x 1 cm

**egg mass**

SCAT WIDTH

**Habitat:** Cold, nonseasonal ponds, streams, and other water sources. In summer, may be found in meadows well away from water.

**Similar species:** Nuptial pad (enlarged pad for holding female during mating) separates male from other hopping amphibians. Differs from toads by more webbing between toes, lack of palm tubercles on front feet, and by hopping more and at longer distances. Larger than chorus frog.

**Other sign:** Softball-size egg masses floating just below water surface.

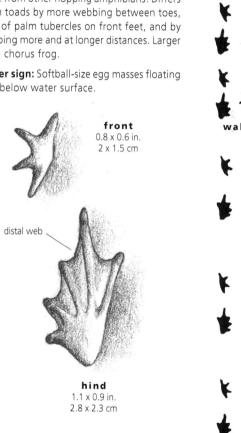

**front**
0.8 x 0.6 in.
2 x 1.5 cm

distal web

**hind**
1.1 x 0.9 in.
2.8 x 2.3 cm

**walk**

**hop**

*FRONT TRACK LENGTH*

*FRONT TRACK WIDTH*

# Bullfrog
*Rana catesbeiana*

Softball-size frog, 4–8 inches (10–20 cm) long. Brownish green to green, becoming light green on head. Legs banded with dark brown to green; small spots on back. Fold of skin around eye and large exposed eardrum.

**Track:** Four toes on front foot and five on hind. Front feet face in. Three hind toes face in; remaining two face forward or out. Webbing, found only on hind feet, is distal, extending most of the way out to the toe tips. In a clear track, a male's toe 2 (thumb) on front foot appears thicker at base.

**Trail:** Hopping stride is 24 inches (60 cm). May easily hop 72 inches (180 cm).

**scat**
1.5 x 0.4 in.
3.8 x 1 cm

*SCAT WIDTH*

**Scat:** Brown to black, with slightly tapered ends.

**Habitat:** Permanent and (usually) quiet water with dense growth of aquatic plants, especially cattails, in plains, woodlands, and forest.

**Similar species:** Differs from toads by more webbing between toes, lack of palm tubercles on front feet, and by hopping more and at longer distances. Differs from leopard frog and chorus frogs by larger feet.

**Other sign:** Deposits a globular egg mass.

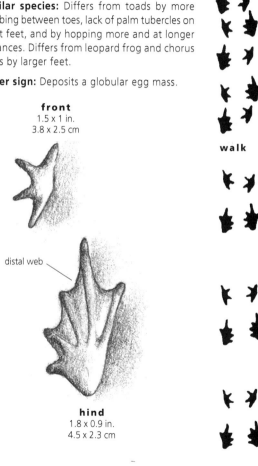

**front**
1.5 x 1 in.
3.8 x 2.5 cm

distal web

**hind**
1.8 x 0.9 in.
4.5 x 2.3 cm

**walk**

**hop**

FRONT TRACK LENGTH

FRONT TRACK WIDTH

# Northern Fence Lizard
*Sceloporus undulatus*

Roughly the size of a roll of Life Savers®; body about 3 inches (7.5 cm), with dry skin and ridged scales. Gray to dark brown above, with black crossbars or longitudinal stripes. Blue patches surrounded by black on side of throat. Considerable subspecies variation.

**Track:** Five relatively long, thin toes on front and hind feet. Hind heel is relatively long. Claws may show.

**Trail:** Trotting stride is about 3 inches (7.5 cm). Hind feet mostly register on top of front feet. Relatively wide straddle. Straight tail drag.

**Scat:** Brown cord, up to six to eight times longer than wide. White nitrogenous material usually found on one end.

**Habitat:** Wide variety of dry habitats, including forests, woodland, and rock outcrops. Shelters in bushes, trees, under rocks, or in logs.

**scat**
1.5 x 0.25 in.
3.8 x 0.6 cm

SCAT WIDTH

**Similar species:** Differs from salamanders by having five narrow toes on front feet and straighter tail drag. Differs from horned lizard by narrower footprint.

**Other sign:** Scuff marks in dust may indicate a dust bath.

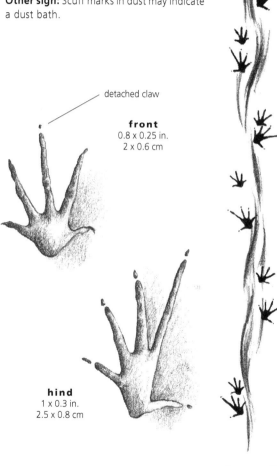

detached claw

**front**
0.8 x 0.25 in.
2 x 0.6 cm

**hind**
1 x 0.3 in.
2.5 x 0.8 cm

**slow walk**

*FRONT TRACK LENGTH*

*FRONT TRACK WIDTH*

# Snapping Turtle
*Chelydra serpentina*

A large to very
large turtle,
average weight
10–30 pounds
(4.5–16 kg).
The robust shell
is lined by three
toothed ridges.
Large head with robust, hooked jaw. Tail
longer than half the shell and toothed on top.

**Track:** Five toes show in front and in hind tracks. Front prints toe in and hind prints may toe out. Feet are relatively broad. Claws robust and often visible. Sometimes the claws are the only visible sign on hard ground.

**Trail:** Walking stride ranges from 5–12 inches (12.5–30 cm). Straddle is wide compared to stride. Tail drag often present.

**Scat:** Lacks well-defined shape. Color is algae green to dark black. Often soft.

**Habitat:** Always near water, including swamps, marshes, lakes, streams, and rivers.

**scat**
1.5 in.
3.8 cm

**Similar species:** Broad trail of five-toed, clawed tracks separates the snapping turtle tracks and trail. Front footprint shows five claws, separating it from the painted turtles.

**Other sign:** Nest in open area where sun warms sand and eggs. Nest may be several inches deep.

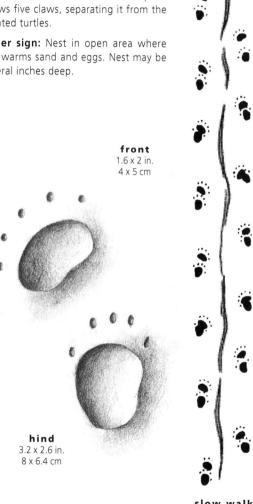

**front**
1.6 x 2 in.
4 x 5 cm

**hind**
3.2 x 2.6 in.
8 x 6.4 cm

**slow walk**

FRONT TRACK LENGTH

FRONT TRACK WIDTH

# Painted Turtle
*Chrysemys picta*

A small turtle with
smooth, unkeeled
shells and patterns
of red, yellows, and
black. Length to 8
inches (20 cm). Females
larger than males.

**Track:** Five toes with claws
show in front and back prints. Claws
longer on front feet and those of the
male's front feet are two to three times
longer than the female's. Outer toe on
hind foot lacks claw. Distal webbing on
front and hind prints.

**Trail:** Walking stride averages 4.5 inches
(11.5 cm) with a straddle of 4 inches
(10 cm). Front feet toe in and hind feet
toe out. Hind footprint registers slightly
behind. Tail drag often visible.

**Scat:** Usually black semiliquid, slightly elongated clumps.

**scat**
0.9 x 0.2 in.
1.3 x 0.5 cm

SCAT WIDTH

**Habitat:** Ponds, lakes, marshes, swamps, streams, and ditches with abundant vegetation.

**Similar species:** Differs from snapping turtles by its narrow straight trail.

**Other sign:** Nests are usually dug in sand in open areas where sun warms eggs.

**front**
0.8 x 0.7 in. without claws
2 x 1.8 cm

**hind**
1.1 x 1 in. without claws
2.8 x 2.5 cm

**walk**

*FRONT TRACK LENGTH*

*FRONT TRACK WIDTH*

# Snakes

various species

**A variety of snakes, from garter snakes (*Thamnophis sirtalis*) to milk snakes (*Lampropeltis triangulum*) to timber (*Crotalus horridus*) and massasauga (*Sistrurus catenatus*) rattlesnakes.**

**Timber Rattlesnake**
*Crotalus horridus*

**Track:** No footprint to describe.

**Trail:** Varies from 1–4 inches (2.5–10 cm) wide. Characterized by side-to-side undulations of the trail. The period, the distance from one curve to the next, varies by species, age, and speed of the snake. Surface material is usually pushed up at the outside of each curve. Gait is either a side-to-side undulation or sidewinding.

**Scat:** Black or brown cord, with constrictions and undulations. White nitrogenous material often attached.

**scat**
4 x 0.4 in.
10 x 1 cm

**shed skin**

SCAT WIDTH

**Habitat:** Varies widely, from water's edge to rock outcrops to dry sand dunes.

**Similar species:** Resembles no other track.

**Other sign:** Shed skin.

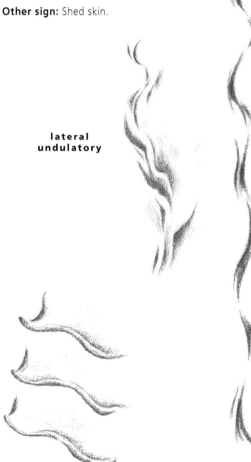

**lateral undulatory**

**sidewinding**

**trail**

# Common Loon
*Gavia immer*

Large-size, long-bodied aquatic bird; average length 24 inches (60 cm). Dark-colored bird with black-and-white checkered back and neck band. Dark greenish head.

**Track:** Three toes showing, toes 2–4 pointing forward. Toe 1 does not register. Toes 2, 3, and 4 have claws and distal webbing.

**Trail:** Walking stride is 10 inches (25 cm) with a 7-inch (18 cm) straddle. Toes turn inward. Foot drag marks usually evident because the loon's legs are placed far back on its body, making walking difficult and causing the loon to drag its feet.

**Scat:** Not known.

**nest**

**Habitat:** Inland lakes and rivers; near shore on Great Lakes.

**Similar species:** Differs from all other aquatic birds by heavy drag marks in trail and relatively long narrow feet.

**Other sign:** Large nest on reeds and brush at edge of water. Eggs appear large in small nest.

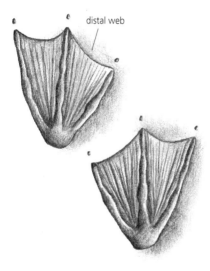

distal web

**feet**
5.25 x 4.3 in.
13.1 x 10.8 cm

**walk**

*TRACK LENGTH*

*HALF TRACK WIDTH*

# White Pelican
*Pelecanus erythrorhynchos*

Large aquatic bird, average length more
than 60 inches (150 cm), with
a wingspan of more
than 8 feet (2.4 m).
White with
black primary
wing feathers.
Large bill
is yellow to
orange.

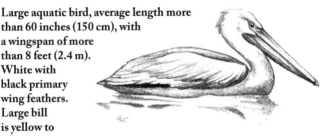

**Track:** Four long, slender toes. Toe 1
offset to side of track. Feet *totipalmate*,
with webbing between all four toes.
Webbing distal and slightly convex
between toes. Claws attached.

**Trail:** Walking stride averages 16 inches
(40 cm). Toes turn inward.

**Scat:** Shapeless, brownish-white mass.

**ground nest**

**Habitat:** Lakes, marshes, and bays. During summer, found in freshwater lakes; in winter, in salt water.

**Similar species:** Differs from all web-footed birds except cormorant by being totipalmate. Differs from cormorant by having attached claws.

**Other sign:** Nests on ground in large island colonies.

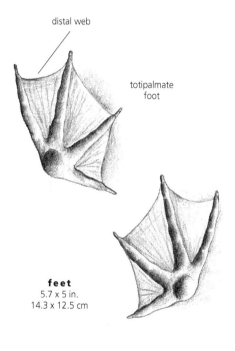

distal web

totipalmate foot

**feet**
5.7 x 5 in.
14.3 x 12.5 cm

**walk**

*TRACK LENGTH*

*HALF TRACK WIDTH*

# Double-crested Cormorant
*Phalacrocorax auritus*

Large aquatic bird, average length more
than 32 inches (80 cm), with a wingspan
of more than 4.3 feet (132 cm). Dark-
colored body with orange throat
patch. Crest of two white feathers
behind eye, which may be difficult to see.

**Track:** Four long, slender toes. Toe 1 offset
to side of track. Toe 4 is
longest. Feet *totipalmate*, with webbing between all four toes. Webbing
distal and slightly convex between
toes. Claws detached.

**Trail:** Walking stride is about 10 inches
(25 cm). Walks awkwardly on land,
with a short stride for its size. Toes
turn inward.

**Scat:** Shapeless, nearly liquid white mass.

**ground nest**

**Habitat:** Great Lakes islands, bays, and cliffs; inland lakes, ponds, and swamps.

**Similar species:** Differs from all web-footed birds except pelican by being totipalmate. Differs from pelican by having detached claws.

**Other sign:** Nests in colonies on ground or in trees. Acidic scat kills trees and ground vegetation.

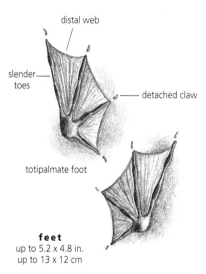

distal web

slender toes

detached claw

totipalmate foot

**feet**
up to 5.2 x 4.8 in.
up to 13 x 12 cm

**walk**

*TRACK LENGTH*

*HALF TRACK WIDTH*

# Green Heron
*Butorides virescens*

Medium-size wading bird, average length 14 inches (36 cm). Male and female similar in overall appearance: blue to greenish body, with reddish-brown neck and yellowish legs.

**Track:** Four toes, toes 2–4 pointing forward. Small proximal web between toes 3 and 4. Footprint is asymmetrical, with toe 1 set to inside of foot axis (drawn through toe 3). On hard ground, metatarsal pad may not show (that is, toes may appear unconnected).

**Trail:** Walking stride about 10 inches (25 cm). Trail is fairly straight and feet point forward.

**Scat:** Semiliquid, predominantly white. Solid cords of scat vary from 1–2 inches (2.5–5 cm) and may contain fish, insects, frogs, and salamanders.

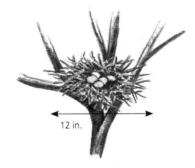

**cough pellet**

12 in.

**nest**
4 to 5 eggs common

**Habitat:** Along ponds, streams, lakes, swamps, and beaches where heavily wooded.

**Similar species:** Smaller version of great blue heron track (6.5 inches/16.5 cm). Differs from other shore-edge tracks by asymmetrical placement of toes.

**Other sign:** Undigested material may be coughed up as pellets.

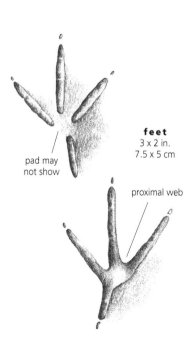

**feet**
3 x 2 in.
7.5 x 5 cm

pad may
not show

proximal web

**walk**

*TRACK LENGTH*

*TRACK WIDTH*

# Great Blue Heron
*Ardea herodias*

Large wading bird, average length 45 inches (113 cm). Male and female similar in overall appearance: gray-blue body, with white neck and yellow beak. Black crown extends on feathers off rear of head.

**Track:** Four toes, toes 2–4 pointing forward. Small proximal web between toes 3 and 4. Footprint is asymmetrical, with toe 1 set to inside of foot axis (drawn through toe 3). Toe 1 is about 1.5 inches (3.8 cm); toe 2 is longer than 1, though shorter than 3 and 4. On hard ground, metatarsal pad may not show (that is, toes may appear unconnected).

**Trail:** Walking stride about 20 inches (50 cm). Trail is fairly straight, and feet point forward.

**cough pellet**

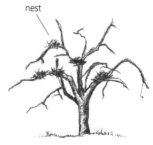

nest

**rookery**

**Scat:** Semiliquid, predominantly white. Solid cords of scat vary from 2–3 inches (5–7.5 cm) in length and contain fish, frogs, salamanders, and even small rodents. Ground beneath nests becomes coated with droppings.

**Habitat:** Frequents backwater eddies along riverbanks and shallow edges of lakes.

**Similar species:** Differs from other shore-edge tracks by large size and asymmetrical placement of toes.

**Other sign:** Large colonies of nests high in trees. Undigested material may be coughed up as pellets.

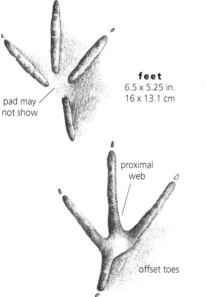

pad may not show

**feet**
6.5 x 5.25 in.
16 x 13.1 cm

proximal web

offset toes

**walk**

# Mute Swan
*Cygnus olor*

Large aquatic bird, length averaging 60 inches (150 cm). Male larger than female. Adult is all white, with an orange bill with a black knob at base. Immature swan has gray plumage. Male and female identically colored. Swims with curved neck and arched wings.

**Track:** Four toes. Toes 2–4, which point forward, usually register. Toe 1 points rearward and only occasionally shows. Distal webbing between toes 2, 3, and 4. Toes 2 and 4 tend to converge slightly near tips. Claws are broad, blunt, and attached to toes. Feet turned in.

**Trail:** Walking stride is about 14 inches (35 cm).

**Scat:** Cord, five to eight times longer than wide. Often greenish and coated with white nitrogen deposits.

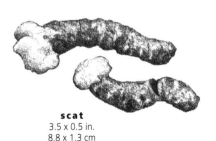

**scat**
3.5 x 0.5 in.
8.8 x 1.3 cm

SCAT WIDTH

**Habitat:** Ponds, lakes, swamps, and slowly flowing streams and rivers, all with emergent vegetation.

**Similar species:** Larger than ducks and geese. Differs from pelican and cormorant by lacking webbing between toes 1 and 2. Larger than gulls; also differing from them by having convergent toes and distal webbing.

**Other sign:** Nests on elevated areas such as cattails, reeds, or roots. Eggs larger than those of Canada goose.

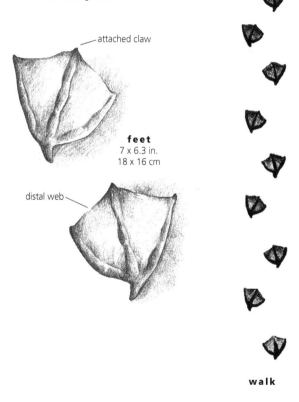

attached claw

**feet**
7 x 6.3 in.
18 x 16 cm

distal web

**walk**

*HALF TRACK LENGTH*

# Ducks
various species

A variety of ducks, from buffleheads (*Bucephala albeola*) to mallards (*Anas platyrhynchos*). Aquatic birds with webbed feet, varying in size from the small bufflehead through mallards to pintails. Length ranges from 14–24 inches (35–60 cm). Large variety in body patterns among species. Males generally more brightly colored than females.

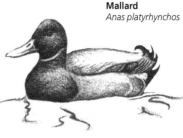

**Mallard**
*Anas platyrhynchos*

**Track:** Four toes. Toes 2–4, which point forward, usually register. Toe 1 points rearward and may not show. Distal webbing between toes 2, 3, and 4. Webbing concave between toes. Toes 2 and 4 tend to converge near tips. Claws are broad, blunt, and attached to toes. Feet turned in.

**Trail:** Walking stride of a mallard (illustrated here) is about 4 inches (10 cm).

**scat**
2 x 0.25 in.
5 x 0.6 cm

SCAT WIDTH

**Scat:** Pencil-size cords, four to eight times longer than wide. Often greenish and coated with white nitrogen deposits.

**Habitat:** Ponds, lakes, marshes, streams, rivers, and bays.

**Similar species:** Tracks smaller than geese and swan. Differ from pelican and cormorant by lacking webbing between toes 1 and 2. Differ from gulls by having convergent toes.

**Other sign:** Nests may be on the ground, in tree cavities, or on floating mats. Eggs roughly the size of chicken eggs, though there may be great variation among species.

distal web

**feet**
2.2 x 2.4 in.
5.5 x 6 cm

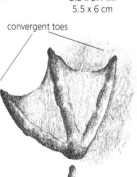

convergent toes

**walk**

*TRACK LENGTH*

*TRACK WIDTH*

# Canada Goose
*Branta canadensis*

Medium-size aquatic bird, average length 30 inches (75 cm). Considerable size variation among subspecies. Black head and neck, with a white chin band. Back is olive brown. Male and female similarly colored.

**Track:** Four toes. Toes 2–4, which point forward, usually register. Toe 1 points rearward and only occasionally shows. Distal webbing between toes 2, 3, and 4. Toes 2 and 4 tend to converge slightly near tips. Claws are broad, blunt, and usually attached to toes. Feet turn in.

**Trail:** Walking stride is about 12 inches (30 cm).

**Scat:** Cord, five to eight times longer than wide. As long as 3.5 inches (8.8 cm). Often greenish and coated with white nitrogenous deposits.

**scat**
3 x 0.4 in.
7.5 x 1 cm

SCAT WIDTH

**Habitat:** Ponds, lakes, marshes, streams, rivers, and bays.

**Similar species:** Larger than most ducks and smaller than swans. Differs from pelican and cormorant by lacking webbing between toes 1 and 2. Larger than gulls and differing from them by having convergent toes and distal webbing.

**Other sign:** Nests on ground, sometimes on cliff ledges, and in abandoned heron and raptor nests. Eggs larger than chicken eggs.

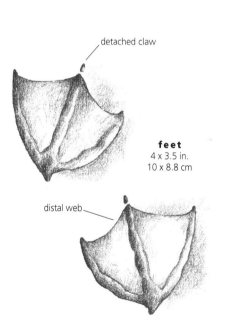

detached claw

**feet**
4 x 3.5 in.
10 x 8.8 cm

distal web

**walk**

FRONT TRACK LENGTH

# Red-tailed Hawk
*Buteo jamaicensis*

Medium-size bird, up to 25 inches (63 cm) in length, with wingspans of 50 inches (125.0 cm). A highly variable, dark-colored hawk with red tail feathers. Light phase has a dark belly band.

**Track:** Four wide, robust toes. Toes 2–4 point forward. Claws are long, sharp, and not attached to the toe print.

**Trail:** Walking stride about 12 inches (30 cm). Hops or runs after prey on the ground. Claws may drag in soft mud, creating a fringe along sides of footprint.

**Scat:** Semiliquid, primarily white with some brown intermixed. Unlike owls, scats is ejected with force, sometimes leaving a trail. Whitish piles and vertical streaks below nests.

**cough pellets**

**Habitat:** Woodland and open country with scattered trees.

**Similar species:** Smaller than eagles but larger than other hawks. Differs from owls by having three toes pointing forward. Differs from geese and swans by lacking webbing. Differs from herons and cranes by having symmetrical feet.

**Other sign:** Cough pellets may be 1.5–4 inches (3.8–10 cm) long.

**walk**

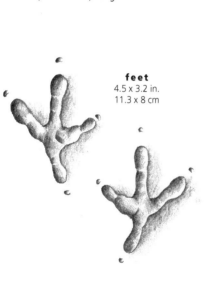

**feet**
4.5 x 3.2 in.
11.3 x 8 cm

*TRACK LENGTH*

*TRACK WIDTH*

# Eagles
two species

Large birds, averaging
35 inches (90 cm) in
length, with wingspans
of 80 inches (200 cm).
Brown bodies. Adult
golden eagle (*Aquila
chrysaetos*) has golden
feathers over head and
neck. Adult bald eagle (*Haliaeetus leucocephalus*) has white
head, neck, and tail feathers.

**Bald eagle**
*Haliaeetus leucocephalus*

**Track:** Four wide, robust toes. Toes
2–4 point forward. Lacks webbing and
metatarsal pad. Claws are long, sharp,
and not attached to the toe print.

**Trail:** Walking stride about 18 inches (45
cm). Golden eagle will run after prey on
the ground.

**Scat:** Semiliquid, primarily white with
some brown intermixed.

**Habitat:** Golden eagle found in mountainous areas and hunts
over open country. Bald eagle usually found near lakes and rivers.

**cough pellet**

**urine stain on rock**

**Similar species:** Larger than hawk's track, which is less than 3 inches (7.5 cm). Differs from owls by having three toes pointing forward. Differs from geese and swans by lacking webbing. Differs from herons and cranes by having symmetrical feet.

**Other sign:** Cough pellets may be 5 × 1.5 inches (12.5 × 3.8 cm). Nests may be 6 feet (2 m) in diameter.

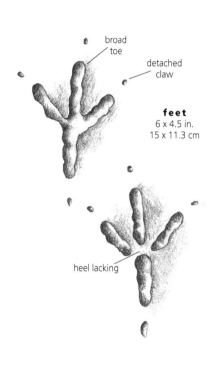

broad toe

detached claw

**feet**
6 x 4.5 in.
15 x 11.3 cm

heel lacking

**walk**

# Ruffed Grouse
*Bonasa umbellus*

**Size comparable to a chicken, 17 inches (43 cm) in length. Mottled brown in color. Black feather ruffs on side of neck. Wide, multibanded tail with dark band near tip.**

**Track:** Four toes, with toes 2–4 pointing forward. Toe 1, relatively short, may not show. Toes are relatively wide and lack webbing. Claws detached. In winter, a fringe of scales makes toes wider. Metatarsal present and may be unattached to toes.

**Trail:** Walking stride is about 9 inches (23 cm). Trail is straight and feet toe in. In deep snow, there can be a 4-inch (10 cm) wide trough. Look for wing marks in the snow as well as body impression under brush and evergreen trees.

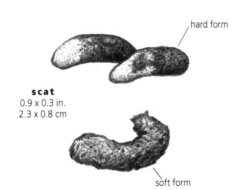

hard form

**scat**
0.9 x 0.3 in.
2.3 x 0.8 cm

soft form

SCAT WIDTH

**Scat:** Light to dark brown, sometimes with white nitrogenous covering. Content includes buds, berries, and sawdust. In winter, deposited in snow nest in large mass of fifty or so scats. May be scattered if roosting in trees.

**Habitat:** Mixed deciduous woodlands with dense understory. Prefers aspen groves.

**Similar species:** Tracks larger than bobwhite. Differs from other forest birds by wide, robust toe size and short toe 1. Grouse trails can be differentiated from those of other forest birds by their short stride.

**Other sign:** Burrow under the snow to roost. Round nests usually 5 inches (13 cm) in diameter made from leaves and brush. Dust baths in sandy areas.

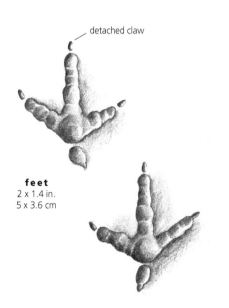

detached claw

**feet**
2 x 1.4 in.
5 x 3.6 cm

**walk**

TRACK LENGTH

TRACK WIDTH

# Ring-necked Pheasant

*Phasianus colchicus*

A large chicken-like bird, males 33 inches (84 cm) and females 21 inches (53 cm) in length. Male brightly colored with green head, mottled brown, black, bronze, and white body. Female is a mottled buffy brown. Male has a long, pointed tail.

**Track:** Four toes, with toes 2–4 pointing forward. Toe 1, relatively short, may not show. Toes are relatively wide and lack webbing. Feet point forward to slightly inward. Metatarsal pad may show and may be unattached from toes.

**Trail:** Walking stride is about 11 inches (28 cm). Narrow trail; toes neither toe in or out.

**scat**
0.8 x 0.4 in.
2 x 1 cm

SCAT WIDTH

**Scat:** Variable bulbous dropping, greenish brown with white ends. Sometimes two or more pieces sticking together.

**Habitat:** Bushy country, woodland edges, farmlands, and windrows.

**Similar species:** Differs from grouse by narrow toes, longer stride, and narrower straddle. Smaller, narrower tracks differentiate from turkey.

**Other sign:** Nest in grass is a shallow depression occasionally lined with some grass.

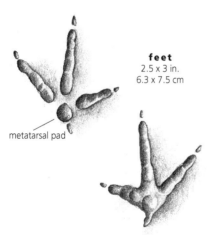

**feet**
2.5 x 3 in.
6.3 x 7.5 cm

metatarsal pad

**walk**

TRACK LENGTH

TRACK WIDTH

# Northern Bobwhite
*Colinus virginianus*

**Size comparable to a small chicken, 9 inches (23 cm) in. length. Mottled reddish brown with a short gray-colored tail. Male with white stripes on face and throat, brownish in female.**

**Track:** Four toes, with toes 2–4 pointing forward. Toe 1, relatively short, may be detached or not show. Toes are relatively wide and lack webbing. Feet point forward to slightly inward. Metatarsal present.

**Trail:** Walking stride is about 6 inches (15 cm). Trail is straight but feet toe in.

**Scat:** Light to dark brown, sometimes with white nitrogenous covering.

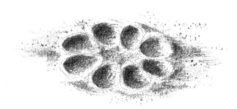

**depressions in dust from chicks**

**scat**
1.4 x 0.2 in.
3.5 x 0.5 cm

SCAT WIDTH

**Habitat:** Tall grasslands, brushlands, open woodlands, and cultivated fields.

**Similar species:** Tracks smaller than grouse. Differs from other forest birds by wide, robust toe size and short toe 1. Bobwhite trails can be differentiated from those of other forest birds by their short strides and wide straddles.

**Other sign:** Ground roost is a circle of shallow body depressions where birds sleep with their heads pointing out. Nest is a shallow depression under "woven" grass with a side entrance.

**walk**

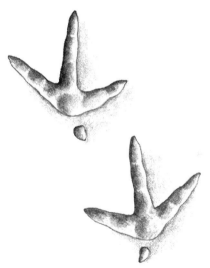

**feet**
1.75 x 1.5 in.
4.4 x 3.8 cm

*TRACK LENGTH*

*TRACK WIDTH*

# Turkey
*Meleagris gallopavo*

Large, ground-dwelling bird. Males average 45 inches (113 cm) and females 35 inches (88 cm) in length. Smaller and more slender than the domesticated Thanksgiving turkey. Male has a dark brown to black body, with white stripes on flight feather; tail feathers are tipped with brownish white. Color of female's feathers is similar but dull. Male also has red *wattles*, folds of skin hanging from the chin.

**Track:** Four broad, robust toes. Toes 2–4 face forward. Hind toe (toe 1) only occasionally registers, and then in a straight line with toe 4. Only the claw or tip of toe 1 registers. Metatarsal pad present, though it may be unattached to toes. Claws narrow and usually attached to toe.

**Trail:** Walking stride 15 inches (38 cm). Foot axis may vary, pointing into the line of travel or turning slightly out.

**scat**
3 x 0.5 in.
7.5 x 1.3 cm

**tracks with scratch marks**

SCAT WIDTH

**Scat:** Solid scat is long, up to 3 inches (7.5 cm), narrow, and brown with greenish-white nitrogenous material on ends. Also produces a soft scat that piles in a shapeless mass on ground.

**Habitat:** Open forest, shrubland, and wooded swamps, in trees with lateral branches for roosting at night.

**Similar species:** Differs from other birds by wide, robust toes. Tracks larger than other ground-dwelling birds. Lacks webbing of ducks and certain other aquatic birds. Separated from eagles by presence (usually) of metatarsal pad. Toes 2 and 4 point forward to a greater degree than those of crane.

**Other sign:** Scratches on ground where turkey digs for seeds, acorns, nuts, and insects.

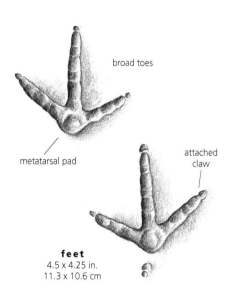

broad toes

metatarsal pad

attached claw

**feet**
4.5 x 4.25 in.
11.3 x 10.6 cm

**walk**

TRACK LENGTH

*HALF TRACK WIDTH*

# Coot
*Fulica americana*

**Medium-size aquatic bird, average length 15 inches (38 cm). Slate-black body, with white beak extending into small brown forehead shield.**

**Track:** Four toes showing, toes 2–4 pointing forward. Toe 1 angles inward. Toes 2, 3, and 4 have fringe of webbing with indented lobes. Long, pointed claws—especially those on toe 1—may be separated from toes.

**Trail:** Walking stride 10 inches (25 cm); tends to wander when walking. Foot axis parallel to line of travel.

**Scat:** White liquid.

**Habitat:** Lakes and ponds having shallow water where reeds and rushes grow.

**Similar species:** Differs from all other aquatic birds by the indented lobes on each toe.

**Other sign:** Floating nest built from cattails, sedges, and rushes, rising several inches above the water.

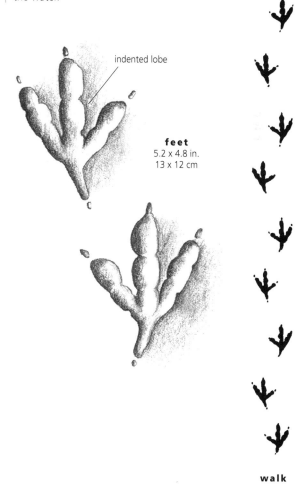

indented lobe

**feet**
5.2 x 4.8 in.
13 x 12 cm

**walk**

# Sandhill Crane
*Grus canadensis*

**Large bird, average length 39 inches (98 cm). Appearance of males and females similar: grayish, with red crown on head and white cheeks and chin.**

**Track:** Four toes, toes 2–4 showing. Outside toes opposed by nearly 180 degrees. Toe 3 is longer than toes 2 and 4. Small proximal web between toes 2 and 3 rarely shows. Claws usually attached to toes, although claw of toe 1 rarely shows. Feet point forward.

**Trail:** Walking stride about 24 inches (60 cm). Often runs, extending its stride. Tracks have a narrow straddle, being nearly in line with each other.

**Scat:** Similar to but smaller than Canada goose. Brown in color, with some vegetation. Can contain bones of small mammals, reptiles, and amphibians.

**Habitat:** Meadows, marshes, grasslands, and fields.

**scat**
2.5 x 0.3 in.
6.3 x 0.8 cm

SCAT WIDTH

**Similar species:** Differs from ducks, geese, swans, and herons by having only small proximal web (if it shows). Differs from large raptors by lacking toe 1.

**Other sign:** Listen for its rattling call, which suggests to some a sound that dinosaurs may have made.

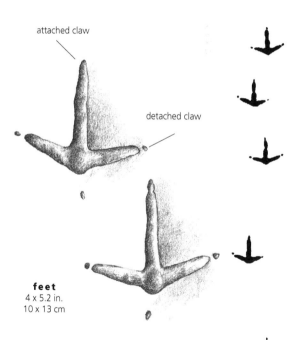

attached claw

detached claw

**feet**
4 x 5.2 in.
10 x 13 cm

**walk**

*TRACK LENGTH*

*HALF TRACK WIDTH*

# Shorebirds
various species

**Avocet**
*Recurvirostra americana*

Many birds, such as avocets (*Recurvirostra americana*), sandpipers, killdeer, curlews, and snipes. Average length varies from 6–18 in. (15–45 cm). All have similar footprints and differentiation is difficult.

**Track:** For avocets (illustrated here) four narrow toes, although toe 1 may not show. Toes 2 to 4 face forward and are nearly symmetrical around toe 3. Outer toe angle often greater than 120 degrees. Small, proximal webbing between toes 2, 3, and 4 may be visible, though curlews and sandpipers have proximal webbing only between toes 3 and 4. Avocets exhibit mesial webbing. Other shorebirds may lack webbing and metatarsal pads. Sandpiper tracks shown here.

**Trail:** Shorebirds are constantly running along the water's edge. Stride varies from 4–20 inches (10–50 cm).

**Scat:** Small and semiliquid. Browns, green and white mixed.

**nest in grass
with twigs**

**Habitat:** Water's edge at lakes, rivers, streams, bays, wastewater treatment plants.

**Similar species:** Differs from songbirds or perching birds by the weak showing of toe 1, which in perching birds is strong and used to grasp branches. Outer toe angle of songbirds is less than 90 degrees. Shorebirds walk, but most songbirds hop.

**Other sign:** Myriad roundish holes where beak pushed into the sand in pursuit of insects.

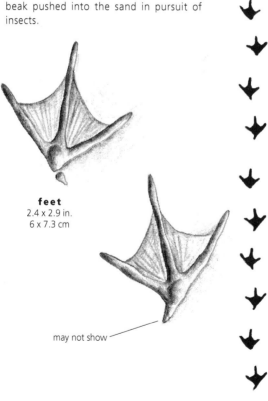

**feet**
2.4 x 2.9 in.
6 x 7.3 cm

may not show

**walk**

*TRACK LENGTH*

*TRACK WIDTH*

# Gulls
various species

Average length
25 inches (63 cm).
Pale-gray back, white
head. Tips of primary
feathers black. Yellow
bill with red spot; pink legs
shown in Herring gull (*Larus
argentatus*) illustrated here
Many species, such as Bona-
parte's, Franklin's, ring-billed,
and herring gulls. Length varies from 11–30 inches (28–76
cm). Gregarious species of open beaches of lakes, oceans, and
rivers.

**Herring gull**
*Larus argentatus*

**Track:** Four toes. Toes 2–4 (forward-pointing) show. Toe 1 may register only slightly or not at all. Webbing relatively straight between toes. Toes 2 and 3 tend to diverge, especially at the tips.

**Trail:** Walking stride of herring gull is about 13 inches (33 cm). Feet turn slightly inward.

**Scat:** Semiliquid. Primarily white, with indistinguishable contents.

**cough pellet**

**Habitat:** Along coast and on inland lakes and rivers. Nests in colonies on ground or cliffs, usually on islands. Nest is made of grass or seaweed. A scavenger, the herring gull is also found at dumps.

**Similar species:** Differ from ducks, swans, and geese by having divergent toes. Smaller than swans and geese. Differ from coot by having webbing between toes.

**Other sign:** Cough pellets containing bones, fish scales, urchin parts, and garbage. Shell fragments from dropping mussel shells onto rocks from high in the air.

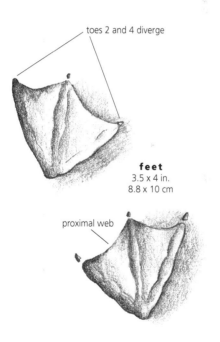

toes 2 and 4 diverge

**feet**
3.5 x 4 in.
8.8 x 10 cm

proximal web

**walk**

TRACK LENGTH

HALF TRACK WIDTH

# Owls
various species

Considerable variation in length, from the saw-whet owl (*Aegolius acadicus*), 8 inches (20 cm), to the short-eared owl (*Asio flammeus*), illustrated here, 15 inches (38 cm), to the great horned owl (*Bubo virginianus*), 25 inches (63 cm). All species have immobile eyes offset by facial disks of feathers. Great variability in appearance among species. Typical body colors are grays, browns, and reddish browns.

**Track:** Four broad toes, with two paired and facing forward. Toe 4 position is not fixed and may face back or out. Lacks webbing and metatarsal pads. Claws long and detached from footprint. Tracks of short-eared owl illustrated.

**Trail:** Walking stride varies considerably among species, from 3–10 inches (7.5–25cm).

**cough pellet**

perch branch

cough pellets

**perch with pellets**

**Scat:** Semiliquid, primarily white.

**Habitat:** Forested areas. Some species, such as barn owls, will readily use human structures.

**Similar species:** Differ from most birds in toes 2 and 3 being paired, nearly parallel, and pointing forward. Differ from woodpeckers by toes being wide and robust, and by toes 1 and 4 being much shorter than toes 2 and 3.

**Other sign:** Cough pellets below a roost. Diameter of cough pellets ranges from 0.25–1 inch (0.6–2.5 cm) and is directly related to the size of the owl. Pellets are shiny and black when fresh but turn gray with age.

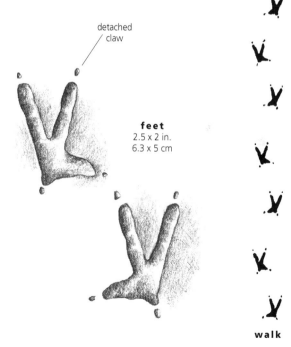

detached
claw

**feet**
2.5 x 2 in.
6.3 x 5 cm

**walk**

TRACK LENGTH

TRACK WIDTH

# Woodpeckers
various species

Considerable variation in size. The northern flicker (*Colaptes auratus*), shown here, is a medium-size woodpecker, slightly larger than the American robin, average length 12 inches (30 cm). Male has brown-barred back, black chest, white rump, and red or black whisker stripe; yellow under wings. Female lacks whisker stripe.

**Track:** Four toes, with two parallel and pointing forward. Toes 1 and 4 point backward and are not equal in length. Strong, rigid tail feathers may show on ground.

**Trail:** Walking stride of the flicker is about 3 inches (7.5 cm). Hopping stride is about 4 inches (10 cm).

**Scat:** Cord, about four or more times longer than wide. Often contains undigested parts of insects.

**Habitat:** Open woodlands, dense forests, and around towns.

SCAT WIDTH

**scat**
1 x 0.25 in.
2.5 x 0.6 cm

**Similar species:** Differ from three-toed woodpecker by presence of toe 1. Differ from other birds their size by having two toes pointing forward.

**Other sign:** Excavates and nests in tree cavities. Does not add bedding material to cavity nest.

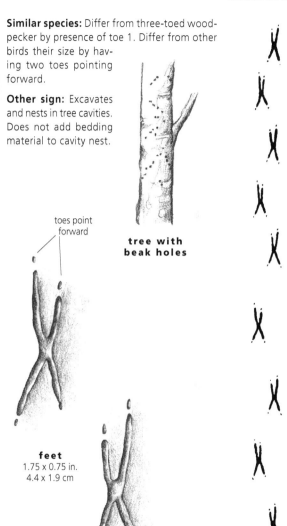

toes point
forward

**tree with
beak holes**

**feet**
1.75 x 0.75 in.
4.4 x 1.9 cm

**walk**

# Blue Jay
*Cyanocita cristata*

Small bird with blue body and white markings on wings. Prominent blue crest and black throat band. Average length about 11 inches (28 cm).

**Track:** Narrow track with four narrow toes, toes 2–4 facing forward and not widely splayed. Toe 1 as long as toes 2, 3, and 4. Toe 1 broader than other toes. Lacks webbing and metatarsal pad. Claws long, especially on toe 1.

**Trail:** Hopping stride is 4–5 inches (10–12.5 cm). Occasionally walks.

**Scat:** Semiliquid, brown to black with white intermixed.

**Habitat:** Woodlands, gardens, and parks.

**Similar species:** Differs from songbirds by larger size and relatively narrow footprint. Smaller and narrower than crows and ravens.

**Other sign:** Nest, on horizontal branch or tree crotch, is compact and occasionally cemented with mud.

**hop**

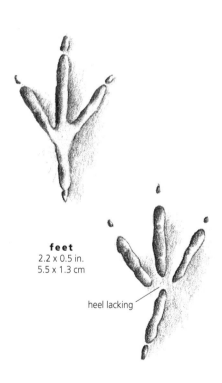

**feet**
2.2 x 0.5 in.
5.5 x 1.3 cm

heel lacking

**walk**

*TRACK LENGTH*

*TRACK WIDTH*

# Crow
*Corvus brachyrhynchos*

**Medium-size, 17 inches (43 cm), black bird with strong beak (smaller than raven's). Sides of tail are parallel in flight, not wedge shaped. Black feet and legs.**

**Track:** Four toes, three facing forward. Toe 1 nearly equals toes 2, 3, and 4. Lacks webbing. Metatarsal pad present but usually does not show. Claws long and often detached from footprint. The footprint length of 2.5 inches (6.3 cm) includes toe 4, which adds 0.7 inch (1.8 cm).

**Trail:** Walking stride varies but is about 5 inches (13 cm). Crows both walk and hop and may run with a long stride.

**Scat:** Semiliquid brown and white; may contain remnants of food from the bird's omnivorous diet.

**cough pellet**

**Habitat:** Roadsides, woodlands, farms, orchards, and lake shores.

**Similar species:** Raven track and trail much larger than crow's. Lacks the paired forward-facing toes of owls. Lacks long toe 1 of hawks.

**Other sign:** Cough pellets up to 1 × 0.4 inch (2.5 × 1 cm). Pellets may contain berries, seeds, nuts, insect parts, and snails, among other items of the bird's varied diet.

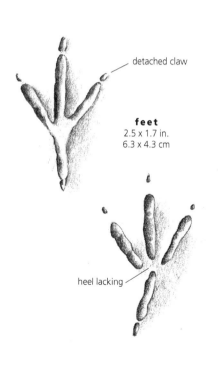

detached claw

**feet**
2.5 x 1.7 in.
6.3 x 4.3 cm

heel lacking

**hop**

**walk**

TRACK LENGTH

TRACK WIDTH

# Common Raven

*Corvus corax*

Large black bird, average length 24 inches (60 cm). Beak wide and robust. Tail is wedge shaped in flight. Size varies considerably, though male is larger than female.

**Track:** Four toes, toes 2–4 facing forward. Length of toe 1 nearly equals toes 2, 3, and 4. Lacks webbing, and metatarsal pad usually does not show. Claws long and detached from footprint.

**Trail:** Walking stride varies considerably, but is about 20 inches (50 cm). Also runs, with a longer stride.

**Scat:** Semiliquid, brown, black, and white; often oily. May contain remnants of the bird's omnivorous diet.

**Habitat:** Especially where carcasses of deer are found, and at garbage dumps. Will beg food from picnickers.

**cough pellet**

**Similar species:** Track and trail of the common crow are diminutive versions of the raven's. Lacks the paired forward-facing toes of owls. Lacks the long toe 1 of hawks. Smaller than eagles.

**Other sign:** Cough pellets up to 3 × 0.5 inch (7.5 × 1.3 cm). Caches food in forks of trees and, often, by burying.

**hop**

detached claw

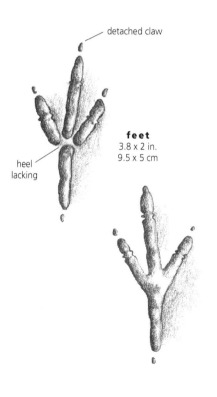

**feet**
3.8 x 2 in.
9.5 x 5 cm

heel
lacking

**walk**

*TRACK LENGTH*

*TRACK WIDTH*

# Opossum
*Didelphis virginiana*

The size of a large
domestic cat,
but more stout,
nearly hairless,
and with a round,
rat-like tail. Weight
varies from 8–14 pounds
(3.5–6.5 kg). Face whitish,
with thin, black-edged ears. Body
is whitish with gray and black hairs
interspersed.

**Track:** Five toes. Hind print is distinctive, with an opposable (like the human thumb) inside toe protruding sideways from other toes and lacking a claw. Outside toe is slightly separated from middle three toes. Front footprint is wider than long and shows long toes that widen slightly toward the end.

**Trail:** Walking stride 18 inches (45 cm). Walking trail often reflects slow movement, with hind footprint registering behind the front. Trail is sloppy, and footprints seldom register directly. Tail drag often shows. Walking pattern occasionally similar to that of the raccoon, where the hind footprint registers beside the front footprint.

scat shape is highly variable

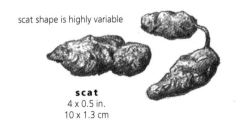

**scat**
4 x 0.5 in.
10 x 1.3 cm

*SCAT WIDTH*

**Scat:** Highly variable shape and size and lack of distinctive form reflect highly variable, omnivorous diet. Single scat may be up to 4 inches (10 cm) long.

**Habitat:** Prefers riparian areas, woodlands, and farmyards. Habitat is not restricted by diet, as the opossum will eat small mammals, birds, eggs, reptiles, amphibians, fish, carrion, fruit, and any garbage it can find.

**Similar species:** Trail may be confused with those of muskrats, woodrats, and domestic rats when a tail drag is present. However, the distinctive hind footprint and large size of the opossum footprint identify its trail.

**Other sign:** Dens in logs, stumps, rock crevices, and dens of other animals.

amble

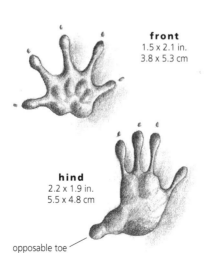

**front**
1.5 x 2.1 in.
3.8 x 5.3 cm

**hind**
2.2 x 1.9 in.
5.5 x 4.8 cm

opposable toe

walk

*FRONT TRACK LENGTH*

*FRONT TRACK WIDTH*

# Shrews
various species

A variety of species, from wandering (*Sorex vagrans*) to short-tailed (*Blarina brevicauda*). Smaller than mice, less than 0.25 ounce (7 g). Long, pointed nose. Minute eyes and ears. Color brown to black, with gray to white belly. Eat mostly insects. The masked shrew (*Sorex cinereus*) is illustrated here.

**Track:** Five slender toes are present on front and hind feet. In clear prints, four interdigital and two proximal pads may be seen.

**Trail:** Hopping stride seldom more than 2 inches (5 cm). The group of tracks is less than 1 inch (2.5 cm) long. Seldom is the stride more than three times the group.

**Scat:** Usually small pellets with tapered ends.

———— tapered ends

**scat**
0.2 x 0.1 in.
0.5 x 0.3 cm

**insect remains**

SCAT WIDTH

**Habitat:** Found everywhere from grasslands to alpine areas. Look for tracks in wet, fine mud of riparian areas or in snow along logs or the edges of buildings. Woodpiles and leaf litter make good homes.

**Similar species:** Differ from mice and voles by having five toes on front foot.

**Other sign:** After eating, leave body parts from insects they have killed. Often burrow just below the surface of the snow, opening tunnels that partially collapse and expose their route. Trails in the snow radiate from holes like spokes of a wheel.

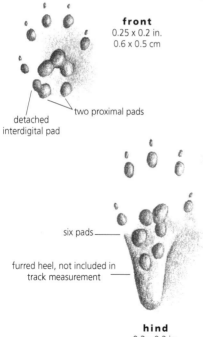

**front**
0.25 x 0.2 in.
0.6 x 0.5 cm

two proximal pads

detached
interdistal pad

six pads

furred heel, not included in
track measurement

**hind**
0.3 x 0.2 in.
0.8 x 0.5 cm

**bound**

FRONT TRACK LENGTH

FRONT TRACK WIDTH

# Red Fox
*Vulpes vulpes*

Jack Russell
terrier–size,
6–15 pounds
(3–7 kg).
Reddish yel-
low, with black
stockings and a
white tip on the tail.
Color phases include
silver, black, cross, and bluish gray. Long, pointed ears and
elongate, pointed muzzle.

**Track:** Claws prominent. One lobe on the leading edge of the interdigital pad. Inside toe slightly larger than outside. A ridge of callus present across interdigital pad, but difficult to detect on hind footprint. Front foot larger than hind.

**Trail:** Trotting stride averages 32 inches (80 cm). Typically uses a trotting gait and occasionally a 2 × 2 trot with body turned to the side. Walks more than coyote, especially in shrubs.

**Scat:** Often has tapered tail. Composition varies. Mouse or rabbit fur, berries, and insects are common. Bird feathers and plant remains often present.

**scat**
2 x 0.6 in.
5 x 1.5 cm

**log**

SCAT WIDTH

**Habitat:** Found in a variety of habitats, from brush to croplands to mixed hard- and soft-wood forest. Prefers edges, where hunting for small mammals is good. Also found in urban areas, where cover is available during the daytime. Not found in dense forests.

**Similar species:** Differs from other canids by having a ridge of callus on the interdigital pad. Track tends to be larger than gray fox and usually shows claws. Differs from bobcat in having only one lobe on the interdigital pad and claws (usually) showing.

**Other sign:** Multiple dens are used each season. Often digs own den. A given den may be used for several years. Look for small bones around den entrance. Scat has a diagnostic musky odor, produced by a musk gland on the top of the tail. Learn to identify this unique foxy odor. Foxes tightrope-walk on narrow logs. May take over woodchuck dens.

**side trot**

**trot**

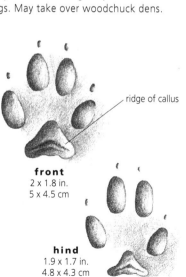

ridge of callus

**front**
2 x 1.8 in.
5 x 4.5 cm

**hind**
1.9 x 1.7 in.
4.8 x 4.3 cm

*FRONT TRACK LENGTH*

*FRONT TRACK WIDTH*

# Gray Fox

*Urocyon cinereoargenteus*

Larger than a miniature poodle, 8–11 pounds (4–5 kg). Body color is pepper-and-salt. A black stripe runs down the back and upper side of tail. Sides are reddish. Tip of tail is black. Long, pointed ears and elongate, pointed muzzle.

**Track:** Small for a canid, somewhat broad and therefore somewhat catlike. Claws, rarely present in track, are very small and sharp, giving the gray fox the ability to climb trees like a cat. Front foot larger than hind.

**Trail:** Generally a trot. Trotting stride averages 24 inches (60 cm). Walks more than coyote.

**Scat:** Often has tapered tail. Composition varies, as the gray fox is opportunistic when feeding. Rabbit fur is most common, followed by fur of other small mammals, berries, and insects. Plant remains are often present.

**scat**
2 x 0.6 in.
5 x 1.5 cm

SCAT WIDTH

**Habitat:** Prefers a mixture of fields, early-stage woodlands, and riparian areas. More common in woodlands than red fox.

**Similar species:** Smaller than coyote. Lacks the ridge of callus on the interdigital pad of the red fox. Differs from coyote in that claws often do not show.

**Other sign:** Seldom digs dens, but makes use of woodpiles, rock outcrops, hollow trees, and brush piles. Look for small bones around den entrances.

**side trot**

**trot**

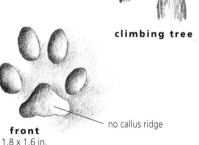

**climbing tree**

no callus ridge

**front**
1.8 x 1.6 in.
4.5 x 4 cm

**hind**
1.7 x 1.6 in.
4.3 x 4 cm

*FRONT TRACK LENGTH*

*FRONT TRACK WIDTH*

# Eastern Coyote
*Canis latrans*

Larger than border collie, 20–25 pounds (9–11 kg). Male larger than female. Color varies from completely gray to tan to rust. Long, pointed ears and long, narrow muzzle.

**Track:** Claws usually present. One lobe on the leading edge of the interdigital pad. Inside toe slightly larger than outside. Front foot larger than hind.

**Trail:** Trotting stride averages 41 inches (94 cm). Often uses a trot with body turned to the side, leaving a 2 × 2 track pattern. Often lopes, leaving a C-shaped pattern.

**Scat:** Varies from pure black animal protein to mostly hair with some bones. Tips tapered into long tails.

**Habitat:** An animal of the open brush country, the coyote digs its den on exposed hilltops or ridges with a view of surrounding area. Where persecuted, may den in a more secluded location.

**Similar species:** Even adult track is smaller than that of a wolf pup. Track may overlap in size with red fox, but lacks callus ridge

**scat**
3 x 0.6 in.
7.5 x 1.5 cm

SCAT WIDTH

of red fox. Track larger than gray fox, and usually shows claws. Differs from bobcat by showing claws and by having one lobe on leading edge of interdigital pad.

**Other sign:** Marks territory with urine and scat piles. Scat pile locations may be used repeatedly. Uses feet to scratch near scat piles, spreading odor from scat and foot glands to identify territory.

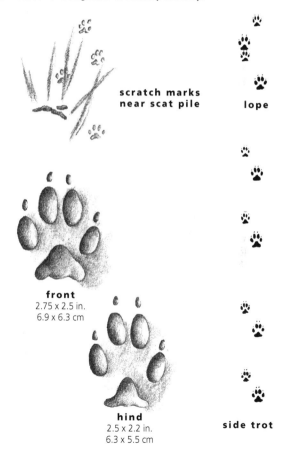

**scratch marks near scat pile**

**front**
2.75 x 2.5 in.
6.9 x 6.3 cm

**hind**
2.5 x 2.2 in.
6.3 x 5.5 cm

**lope**

**side trot**

*FRONT TRACK LENGTH*

*FRONT TRACK WIDTH*

# Gray Wolf
*Canis lupus*

Larger than German shepherd, probably less than 100 pounds (45 kg). Male larger than female. Color varies from completely black to gray. Short, rounded ears and short, wide, blocky muzzle. The wolf apparently recolonizing the Northeast from Canada is a smaller member of the genus.

**Track:** Track about size of a baseball. Claws usually present; one lobe on leading edge of interdigital pad. Inside toe slightly larger than outside. Front foot larger than hind. Given the indefinite origin of wolves, measurements below are approximate and possibly represent upper limits.

**Trail:** Trotting stride averages 62 inches (155 cm). Often uses a C-shaped gallop or a trot with the body turned to the side, leaving a 2 × 2 pattern.

**Scat:** Varies from pure black, toothpaste-like animal protein to mostly hair with some bones. Tips tapered into long tails.

**scat**
4 x 1.25 in.
10 x 3.2 cm

SCAT WIDTH

**Habitat:** Found in all habitats. Tends to use cover when possible, moving in forest or at forest-meadow edge.

**Similar species:** Track larger than other canids. At 60 days of age, track larger than adult coyote's. Differs from mountain lion by having one lobe on the leading edge of the interdigital pad and usually showing claws. Differs from wolverine and bear by having only four toes, with the large toe on the inside.

**Other sign:** The alpha wolf, dominant member of the pack, marks its territory by urinating on raised objects along the trail. Blood observed in the female's urine stain during January or February may indicate readiness to breed. Scratch marks beside urine stains or scat are territorial markings and are usually made with hind feet.

**side trot**

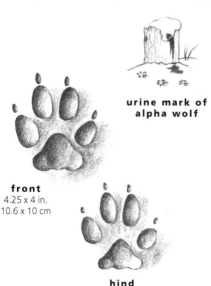

**urine mark of alpha wolf**

**front**
4.25 x 4 in.
10.6 x 10 cm

**hind**
3.75 x 3.25 in.
9.4 x 8.1 cm

**gallop**

*FRONT TRACK LENGTH*

*HALF FRONT TRACK WIDTH*

# Bobcat

*Lynx rufus*

Size of a border collie, 13–35 pounds (6–16 kg). Males larger than females. Overall color reddish to yellowish brown, with dark spots or streaks and whitish underside. Ears have tufts at tips. Back of ears and top of tail tip black. Tail is short or "bobbed," about 4 inches (10 cm) long.

**Track:** Front track is round or wider than long. Hind track may be longer than wide. Claw impressions are usually absent. Toes form a slight arc, and toe 3 leads. The leading edge of the interdigital pad has two lobes. Inside toe distinctly larger than outside toe.

**Trail:** Walking stride is about 20 inches (50 cm). Usually walks, but bounds with hind feet placed side by side when chasing prey. Winter trails often show random vertical leaps, perhaps signaling that the bobcat has jumped after a flying bird.

**Scat:** Tends to be constricted and, if dry, separates at constrictions into segments. Dry scat falls apart. Ends usually blunt. Scat from a fresh kill may form a cord of uniform diameter.

broken constriction

**scat**
3 x 0.8 in.
7.5 x 2 cm

SCAT WIDTH

**Habitat:** Prefers dense cover of swamps and forests, especially with rocky ledges. Open agricultural land is not used. Rock piles, caves, and high rocky ledges are important for bearing young.

**Similar species:** Differs from coyote and other canids by lacking claws, having two lobes on the leading edge of the interdigital pad, and having toe 3 substantially leading. Substantially smaller than both mountain lion and lynx.

**Other sign:** Scent marks made by urine, scat, and anal glands. Scrapes dirt over urine and scat. Caches food by burying.

**walk**

**vertical
leap from
hind feet**

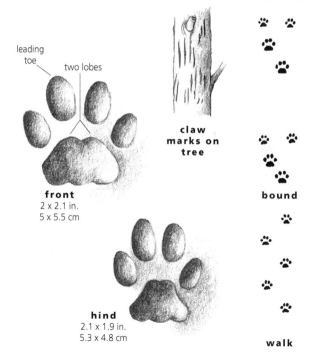

leading
toe

two lobes

**front**
2 x 2.1 in.
5 x 5.5 cm

**claw
marks on
tree**

**bound**

**hind**
2.1 x 1.9 in.
5.3 x 4.8 cm

**walk**

*FRONT TRACK LENGTH*

*FRONT TRACK WIDTH*

# Canada Lynx
*Lynx (Felis) canadensis*

Size of or just smaller than a border collie, with male averaging 22 pounds (10 kg) and female 19 pounds (9 kg). Very long legs and big feet. Reddish to yellowish brown overall, with dark spots or streaks and whitish underside. Ears have tufts at tips. Tail tip is black on top and bottom. Tail is short or bobbed, about 4 inches (10 cm) long.

**Track:** Diameter of a softball and indistinct because the feet are mostly covered with hair and because pads are reduced in size. Feet are large, for better support on snow.

**Trail:** Walking stride is about 28 inches (70 cm). Walking gaits are common, but lynx does trot more than bobcat. Winter trails often show random vertical leaps, perhaps signaling that the lynx has jumped after a flying bird.

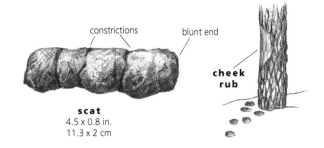

constrictions          blunt end

**cheek rub**

**scat**
4.5 x 0.8 in.
11.3 x 2 cm

SCAT WIDTH

**Scat:** Tends to be constricted and, if dry, separates at constrictions into segments. Ends blunt. Dry scat falls apart. Scat from a fresh kill may form a cord of uniform diameter.

**Habitat:** Found in dense conifer forests interspersed with rocky ledges and downed timber, both of which are used for security and denning. Forest edges, which provide food for the lynx's major prey, snowshoe hare, are critical.

**Similar species:** Track differs from other felids by being inherently indistinct. Interdigital pad is relatively small when compared to bobcat and mountain lion—check closely. Differs from canids by two lobes on interdigital pad and claws not showing.

**Other sign:** Birth dens occur in hollow logs, stumps, and clumps of timber. Adult lynx does not cover scat. Lynx scent marks (urinates) up to twenty-five times per mile.

**fast trot**

**vertical leap from hind feet**

**trot**

**walk**

FRONT TRACK LENGTH

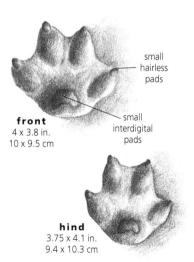

small hairless pads

**front**
4 x 3.8 in.
10 x 9.5 cm

small interdigital pads

**hind**
3.75 x 4.1 in.
9.4 x 10.3 cm

*HALF FRONT TRACK WIDTH*

# Mountain Lion
*Puma concolor*

Larger than an Irish wolfhound, with male averaging 145 pounds (66 kg) and female about 120 pounds (54 kg). Color gray to red, often called tawny, with whitish underside. Back of ears and tip of tail black to brown. Tail is more than half the length of the body. Also called cougar or puma. May be reestablishing in the Great Lakes; track verification needed—photos or casts.

**Track:** Track diameter of a baseball. Front track round or wider than long, and hind track longer than wide. Claw impressions are usually absent. Toes form a slight arc, and toe 3 leads. Leading edge of the interdigital pad has two lobes. Inside toe distinctly larger.

**Trail:** Walking stride is about 40 inches (100 cm). Usually walks, but bounds with hind feet placed side by side when chasing prey.

**Scat:** Scat from a fresh kill may form a cord of uniform diameter with very slight constrictions; ends usually blunt. As the carcass a lion feeds on dries out, the lion's scat tends to develop constrictions, eventually falling apart when diet becomes very dry.

**scat**
4 x 1.25 in.
10 x 3.1 cm

SCAT WIDTH

**Habitat:** Habitat is that of its main prey, deer. Open woodlands with rock ledges and grass (for deer) preferred. Often found in riparian zones with trees.

**Similar species:** Track differs from wolf by the presence of two lobes on the leading edge of the interdigital pad, by having toe 3 substantially leading, and by usually not showing claws. Differs from wolverine and bears by having only four toes and large toe inside.

**Other sign:** Often buries scat by scraping dirt over it with front feet. Scraped ground material may conceal food caches. Male will rake up football-size patches of brush and urinate on them to mark home range.

**Comments:** Breeding populations not known from area. Proof of non-feral or non-escaped animals is needed.

**scraped ground around scat**

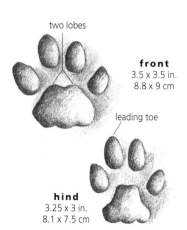

two lobes

**front**
3.5 x 3.5 in.
8.8 x 9 cm

leading toe

**hind**
3.25 x 3 in.
8.1 x 7.5 cm

**bound**

**walk**

*FRONT TRACK LENGTH*

*FRONT TRACK WIDTH*

# Black Bear
*Ursus americanus*

Calf-size bear, female averaging 120 pounds (54 kg) and male about 300 pounds (135 kg). Male grows faster and obtains larger size than female. Color varies from black to brown to blond to red.

**Track:** Claws on front foot, seldom longer than toes, are usually present. Little toe is set back from rest of toes. Hind print has a large, humanlike heel. Outside toe is larger than others.

**Trail:** Walking stride 35–40 inches (88–100 cm). Often ambles, a fast walk where the hind foot oversteps the front. Gait is pigeon-toed. Lopes in a C-shaped pattern or a side gallop.

**Scat:** Normally contains vegetation and is sweet smelling. When the bear is feeding on carcasses, scat varies from black to brown, with mostly hair and some bones. Ants often found in scat. Tips have a short taper or are blunt.

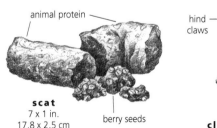

animal protein

**scat**
7 x 1 in.
17.8 x 2.5 cm

berry seeds

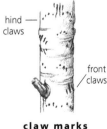

hind claws

front claws

**claw marks on tree**

SCAT WIDTH

**Habitat:** Forest, seldom venturing far into wide openings. Thick understory vegetation and abundant food sources are critical.

**Similar species:** Differs from mountain lion and wolf by having five toes and well-developed heel on hind footprint. Differs from wolverine by having toes tightly packed and having a wedge-shaped interdigital pad.

**Other sign:** Claws trees, rips open logs, digs into ant piles, and turns over rocks and scat as it looks for insects.

side lope

lope

amble

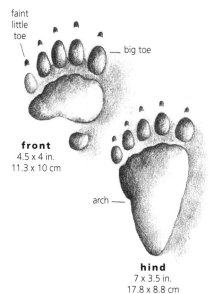

faint little toe

big toe

**front**
4.5 x 4 in.
11.3 x 10 cm

arch

**hind**
7 x 3.5 in.
17.8 x 8.8 cm

*FRONT TRACK LENGTH*

*HALF FRONT TRACK WIDTH*

# Raccoon
*Procyon lotor*

Stocky, smaller than a collie, with broad head and bushy tail. Male averages 18 pounds (8 kg) and female 16 pounds (7 kg). Gray to black overall, with black rings on the tail and a black mask on a white face.

**Track:** Five slender toes, slightly bulbous on the ends. Tracks resemble small human hands and feet. Hind foot has a long, naked heel.

**Trail:** Walking stride averages 27 inches (68 cm). Roll of hips during walk causes hind foot to register beside the opposite front print. C-shaped gallop is common.

**Scat:** Highly variable, but often black, even-diameter cord with blunt ends. Often contains crayfish or fruit. Deposited singly or in dung heaps containing scat from perhaps several individuals. *Caution:* Scat may carry a parasite that is potentially fatal to humans. Do not smell scat, and wash hands after touching.

**Habitat:** River and stream drainages are prime habitats, but storm drains in cities may also provide refuge. Woodpiles in and around towns.

**scat**
3 x 0.75 in.
7.5 x 1.9 cm

SCAT WIDTH

**Similar species:** Differs from bear by having smaller tracks and having slender toes. Differs from river otter by lack of webbing. Larger than mink.

**Other sign:** Digs holes in streambanks to get at crayfish. Leaves piles of crayfish skeletons and claws. Digs for worms in lawns.

**sign left while fishing for crayfish**

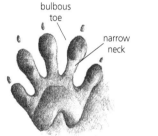

bulbous toe

narrow neck

**front**
2.5 x 2.5 in.
6.3 x 6.3 cm

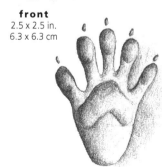

**hind**
4 x 2.3 in.
10 x 5.8 cm

**gallop**

**walk**

*FRONT TRACK LENGTH*

*FRONT TRACK WIDTH*

# Weasels
*Mustela* species

**Long-tailed weasel**
*M. frenata*

Three species,
with long,
slender bodies,
varying in size from a
regular to a foot-long hotdog. Pointed, flat skull with
small ears. Males up to twice as large as females. Largest
males weigh about 1 pound (0.45 kg). Overall color is brown,
with a white belly. In winter, northern individuals turn
entirely white. Hairy, slender tail. The small least weasel (*M. nivalis*) lacks the black tip on the tail found in the ermine (*M. erminea*) and the long-tailed weasel (*M. frenata*), shown here.

**Track:** Wide track. Five toes, in 1-3-1 grouping. Little toe, on inside of foot, often does not register. Interdigital pad chevron shaped. Heel seldom shows. Difficult to distinguish between species.

**Trail:** Galloping stride varies from 8–30 inches (20–75 cm). Side-by-side tracks, when examined closely, show one track slightly in front of the other—a gallop. In snow, a drag mark may be found between front and hind prints, sometimes forming a dumbbell shape. The dumbbell shape indicates fast movement, with hind foot overstepping front track.

**Scat:** Long, slender cord, usually with black, toothpaste-like animal protein or hair. Cord tends to fold back on itself. Tapered at both ends.

folded back ⸺

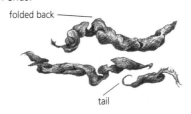

**scat**
1.5 x 0.1 in.
3.5 x 0.3 cm

tail

SCAT WIDTH

**Habitat:** Prefer dense, low ground cover to open areas. Found in habitats where their prey, rodents, are abundant. Trails often lead from one rodent den to another. Travel in snow and ground burrows of other mammals.

**Similar species:** Differ from other mustelids by their smaller size and the drag mark commonly located between twin track patterns in the snow.

**Other sign:** Routes seldom follow a straight line, often having many sharp turns. Scat often deposited on raised objects.

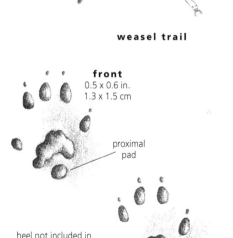

dumbbell shape

erratic route

**weasel trail**

front
0.5 x 0.6 in.
1.3 x 1.5 cm

proximal pad

heel not included in track measurement

**hind**
0.6 x 0.7 in.
1.5 x 1.8 cm

foot drag

**gallop**

**2 x 2 lope**

FRONT TRACK LENGTH

FRONT TRACK WIDTH

# Marten
*Martes americana*

Size of a small
house cat,
but slender,
1–4 pounds
(0.5–2 kg). Male
20 percent larger than
female. Pointed, flat
skull with small ears. Overall
color golden brown, with orange to yellow chest patch. Edges
of ears are white. Hairy, slender tail.

**Track:** Five toes, in 1-3-1 grouping. Little toe, on the inside of foot, sometimes does not register. Interdigital pad is a chevron. Proximal pad may show in front footprint. Heel often shows. Feet are well furred in winter, making tracks indistinct.

**Trail:** Gallop stride averages 22 inches (55 cm). Mostly gallops; a variety of 2 × 2, 3 × 3, and 4 × 4 patterns will be found.

**Scat:** Long, slender cord, tending to fold back on itself. Black or brown in color, occasionally with hair. Tapered at both ends.

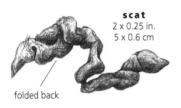

**scat**
2 x 0.25 in.
5 x 0.6 cm

folded back

*SCAT WIDTH*

**climbs tree,
jumps out**

**Habitat:** Old-growth forest, but adaptable to many forest habitats. Prefers mature conifer and mixed forests. Needs tall, hollow, or broken trees for denning. Found near its prey, squirrels and red-backed voles.

**Similar species:** Differs from weasel by its larger size. Lacks the webbed toes of the mink. Also differs from mink by use of terrestrial habitat. Smaller than fisher and occupies areas with deeper snow.

**Other sign:** Frequently burrows beneath snow and climbs up trees; look for tracks that end at a tree trunk. Scratch marks show where stomach was dragged over objects that protrude from the ground or snow to scent mark.

**4 x 4 gallop**

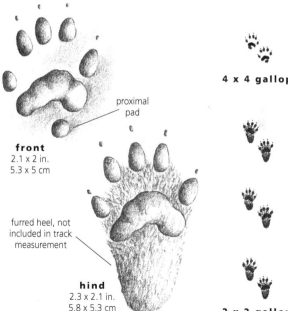

proximal pad

**front**
2.1 x 2 in.
5.3 x 5 cm

furred heel, not included in track measurement

**hind**
2.3 x 2.1 in.
5.8 x 5.3 cm

**2 x 2 gallop**

FRONT TRACK LENGTH

FRONT TRACK WIDTH

# Mink
*Mustela vison*

Size of a small
domestic cat,
but slender,
1.5–3.5 pounds
(0.7–1.5 kg). Male
10 percent larger than
female. Pointed, flat skull
with small ears. Overall color is dark brown,
with white spots on chin and chest. Hairy, slender tail. Webbing occurs between the toes.

**Track:** Five toes, in 1-3-1 grouping. Little toe, on the inside of foot, sometimes does not register. Webbing shows between toes in tracks; look carefully. Interdigital pad chevron shaped. Proximal pad may show in front footprint. Heel seldom shows.

**Trail:** Bounding stride averages 14 inches (35 cm). Bounds more than weasels, but a gallop, averaging 20 inches (50 cm), is also common.

**Scat:** Long, slender cord, usually tending to fold back on itself. Black or brown in color, occasionally with hair. Tapered at both ends. Often contains remains of fish or crayfish. May be oily and smell fishy. Fish oil keeps scat composed of fish scales from

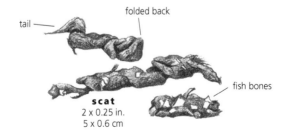

tail — folded back

**scat**
2 x 0.25 in.
5 x 0.6 cm

fish bones

SCAT WIDTH

falling apart until oil evaporates, then scales scatter on the ground.

**Habitat:** River- and streambanks. Seldom far from water.

**Similar species:** Differs from other small mustelids by having more webbing between toes. Larger than weasels. Use of aquatic habitat is an important clue for separation from marten. Tracks and trail much smaller than otter's.

**Other sign:** Mink make "post offices," repeated scat deposits on logs exposed above water's edge. Strong, musky, almost skunk-like odor from anal scent glands.

**fast walk**

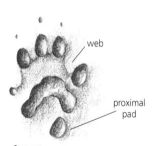

**front**
1.7 x 1.8 in.
4.3 x 4.5 cm

**hind**
1.8 x 1.9 in.
4.5 x 4.8 cm

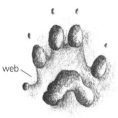

**bound**

FRONT TRACK LENGTH

FRONT TRACK WIDTH

# Fisher

*Martes pennanti*

Larger than a large domestic cat but slender, 7.5–18 pounds (3–8 kg). Male larger than female. Pointed, flat skull with small ears. Color is dark brown. Long bushy tail.

**Track:** Five toes, in 1-3-1 grouping. Little toe, on the inside of foot, sometimes does not register. Interdigital pad chevron shaped. Proximal pad may show in front footprint. Heel seldom shows. Claws short. Feet are not well furred, which in winter makes toes appear clearly in tracks.

**Trail:** Galloping stride averages 28 inches (70 cm). Mostly gallops, but walking, 3 × 3 lope, 1 × 2 × 1 lope, and 2 × 2 gallop patterns are also common.

**Scat:** Only mustelid scat that frequently contains porcupine quills. Long, slender cord, usually tending to fold back on itself. Black or brown in color, occasionally with hair. Tapered at both ends.

**Habitat:** Old-growth forest, especially among conifers and large timber, and in swamp areas. Upland hardwood stands where porcupines den. Will use young forest stands following

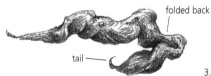

folded back

tail

**SCAT WIDTH**

**scat**
3.5 x 0.5 in.
8.8 x 1.3 cm

fire or timber harvest. Avoids open areas without overhead cover, but will travel on roads and trails.

**Similar species:** Lacks the webbed toes of the mink. Differs from mink by habitat and use of terrestrial sites. Larger than mink and marten and occupies areas of shallower snow. Smaller than wolverine and makes more frequent use of trees for walkways and nests.

**Other sign:** Porcupine skins turned inside out. Snow trails may reveal frequent trips up trees. Walks on logs to avoid deep snow. Drags stomach over objects that protrude from the ground or snow to scent mark, leaving scratches. Travels on packed trails of snowshoe hare.

**1 x 2 x 1 lope**

**3 x 3 lope**

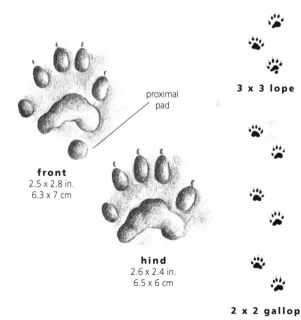

proximal pad

**front**
2.5 x 2.8 in.
6.3 x 7 cm

**hind**
2.6 x 2.4 in.
6.5 x 6 cm

**2 x 2 gallop**

FRONT TRACK LENGTH

FRONT TRACK WIDTH

# River Otter
*Lontra (Lutra) canadensis*

Body and tail form a
4-foot-long cylinder
that tapers to a hairy,
pointed tail. Weight
varies from 10–30 pounds
(5–14 kg). Male slightly larger than female.
Overall color a rich, dark brown, with silver-
brown belly. Webbed toes on front and hind feet.

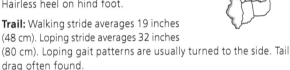

**Track:** Large webbed foot is diagnostic,
but look closely because webbing may
be difficult to see. Hind foot is very wide.
Five toes, in 1-3-1 grouping. Little toe,
on the inside of foot, sometimes does
not register. Interdigital pad chevron
shaped. Proximal pad often shows.
Hairless heel on hind foot.

**Trail:** Walking stride averages 19 inches
(48 cm). Loping stride averages 32 inches
(80 cm). Loping gait patterns are usually turned to the side. Tail
drag often found.

**Scat:** Usually contains fish remains, including scales and verte-
brae. The texture is oily and the smell fishy. Fish oil keeps scat
composed of fish scales from falling apart. Scat decomposes as
oil evaporates, eventually falling into a pile of scales.

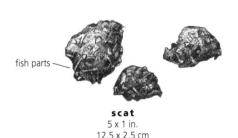

fish parts —

**scat**
5 x 1 in.
12.5 x 2.5 cm

SCAT WIDTH

**Habitat:** River- and streambeds. Lives and nests in bank burrows but may also nest in logjams. In spring, while looking for a mate, travels overland, often several miles from water sources.

**Similar species:** Differs from other species by webbing and large, wide hind foot.

**Other sign:** Loose dirt banks show where otters have rolled to dry off. Rolls around tufts of grass, twisting them into scent posts. Travels by sliding down banks and along level snow and over ice-covered lakes.

**side lope**

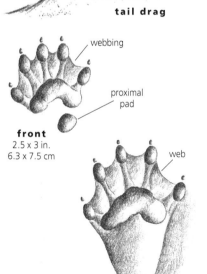

**tail drag**

webbing

proximal pad

**front**
2.5 x 3 in.
6.3 x 7.5 cm

web

**hind**
3 x 3.6 in.
7.5 x 9 cm

**bound**

# Badger

*Taxidea taxus*

Jack Russell–size, about 18 pounds (8 kg), with flat body, long hair, and long, shovel-like claws. Male 25 percent larger than female. Color varies from silver-gray to yellowish brown on back, with white belly. Feet are black or dark brown. White stripe down nose, with black markings on sides of face. Short tail.

**Track:** Diameter of a golf ball, with long front claws, nearly as long as rest of footprint. Five toes, in 1-3-1 grouping. Little toe, on the inside of foot, sometimes does not register. Interdigital pad chevron shaped. Proximal pad often shows. Front footprint larger than hind.

**Trail:** Walking stride averages 14 inches (35 cm). Walking is most common, but trotting, with a stride of 29 inches (73 cm), occurs frequently.

**Scat:** Seldom found because deposited belowground in burrows. Similar to but smaller than coyote scat, without tapered ends.

**scat**
3 x 0.8 in.
7.5 x 2 cm

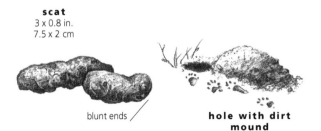

blunt ends

**hole with dirt mound**

*SCAT WIDTH*

**Habitat:** Open grasslands preferred. Areas with large populations of prey, which includes ground squirrels and prairie dogs.

**Similar species:** Differs from all other species by long claws on front foot and disproportionately small hind foot.

**Other sign:** Fresh excavations of large amounts of dirt from burrowing rodent holes indicates hunting activity, especially if excavated material includes large clods or rocks. Freshly widened burrow entrances may have a slightly elliptical shape. The presence of coyote and badger tracks together indicates cooperative hunting.

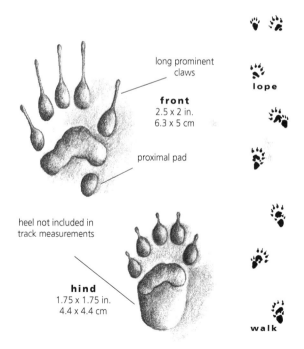

long prominent claws

**front**
2.5 x 2 in.
6.3 x 5 cm

proximal pad

heel not included in track measurements

**hind**
1.75 x 1.75 in.
4.4 x 4.4 cm

lope

walk

FRONT TRACK LENGTH

FRONT TRACK WIDTH

# Striped Skunk
*Mephitis mephitis*

Black-and-white mustelid, size of a domestic cat, with triangular head. Weight varies from 4–10 pounds (2–5 kg). Male is slightly larger than female. Flat, wide, bushy tail with white hair on top. Long, curved claws for digging.

**Track:** Half-dollar size, with long front claws. Hind track looks like a little human footprint. Five toes in 1-3-1 grouping. Little toe, on the inside of foot, sometimes does not register. Interdigital pad chevron shaped. Proximal pad often shows. Hairless heel on hind foot.

**Trail:** Walking stride averages 12 inches (30 cm). Meanders and stops often when walking, leaving extra footprints in trail. Lope may be turned to the side or straight forward.

**Scat:** Cylindrical with blunt ends. Lacks the long taper and tendency to fold back on itself of other mustelid scat. May be composed entirely of insect parts.

blunt

**scat**
5 x 0.75 in.
12.5 x 1.9 cm

fanged puncture

**chewed eggs**

SCAT WIDTH

**Habitat:** Not habitat-specific. Lives where burrows, cavities, or tunnels are present, including in and around buildings. Presence of insects and small mammals is critical to habitat selection.

**Similar species:** Differs from other species by having long, wide claws on the front foot. Smaller than badger, with front and hind feet similar in size. Some authors put skunks in their own family separate from weasels.

**Other sign:** Smell of skunk musk identifies nests and burrows. Tears apart nests of small mammals. Bird eggs show four fang punctures around larger hole in shell.

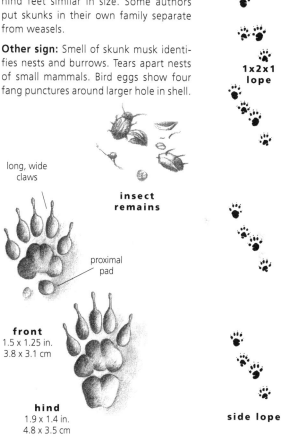

**1 x 2 x 1
lope**

long, wide
claws

**insect
remains**

proximal
pad

**front**
1.5 x 1.25 in.
3.8 x 3.1 cm

**hind**
1.9 x 1.4 in.
4.8 x 3.5 cm

**side lope**

*FRONT TRACK LENGTH*

*FRONT TRACK WIDTH*

# Eastern Cottontail Rabbit

*Sylvilagus floridanus*

**Small rabbit with large ears and feet, small white tail. Averages about 3 pounds (1.4 kg). Color pepper-and-salt or gray and white.**

**Track:** Toes asymmetrical around foot axis. Track indistinct because the foot is completely haired and lacks pads. Occasionally claws will register; these may be the only sign of a hopping rabbit. Hind footprint about two times longer than front.

**Trail:** Hopping stride is about 3 feet (90 cm). Most of the time rabbits hop, but walking patterns will occasionally be observed.

**Scat:** Dry scat is a slightly flattened sphere. Produces a black, semiliquid scat that is usually re-ingested to utilize remaining nutrients.

**scat**
0.2 in.
0.5 cm

**chewed branch and bud**

*SCAT WIDTH*

**Habitat:** Found wherever there is grass for food and suitable cover, including brush piles, herbaceous and shrubby vegetation, and grasslands. May use dens of other animals for escape cover.

**Similar species:** Differs from snowshoe hare by having shorter heels and smaller overall size.

**Other sign:** Sharp incisors cleanly cut herbaceous vegetation at the height of a sitting rabbit 4–8 inches (10–20 cm). Look for tips of branches with young sprouts chewed off. The cottontail's bed, known as a *form*, is a shallow depression in earth, grass, or snow.

**walk**

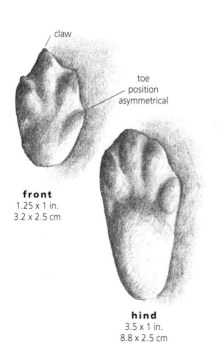

claw

toe
position
asymmetrical

**front**
1.25 x 1 in.
3.2 x 2.5 cm

**hind**
3.5 x 1 in.
8.8 x 2.5 cm

**claws only
on hard
ground**

**hop**

FRONT TRACK LENGTH

FRONT TRACK WIDTH

# White-tailed Jackrabbit
*Lepus townsendii*

Large, slender hare with long ears and feet. Averages about 5 pounds (2 kg). Body color is gray and white to black and white, with white tail. May turn all white in the winter.

**Track:** Toes asymmetrical around foot axis. Track indistinct because foot is completely haired and lacks pads. Claws occasionally will register; on hard ground, they may be the only sign of a footprint. Hind footprint about three times longer than front.

**Trail:** Galloping stride may reach 10 feet (3 m). Tends to gallop rather than bound.

**Scat:** Dry scat is a slightly flattened sphere. Produces a black, semiliquid scat that is usually re-ingested to utilize remaining nutrients.

**Habitat:** Inhabits open areas, from plains grasslands to above tree line in the mountains.

**scat**
0.3 in.
0.8 cm

SCAT WIDTH

**sharp cut grass**

**Similar species:** Track differs from Eastern cottontail by having long shape. Differs from snowshoe hare by its narrow width.

**Other sign:** Sharp incisors cleanly cut herbaceous and woody vegetation at the height of a sitting rabbit, 4–6 inches (10–15 cm). The jackrabbit's nest, known as a *form*, is a shallow depression, usually found under protective cover.

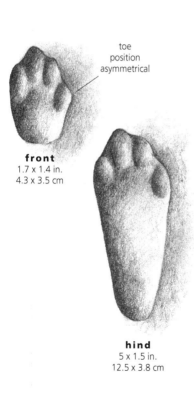

toe position asymmetrical

**front**
1.7 x 1.4 in.
4.3 x 3.5 cm

**hind**
5 x 1.5 in.
12.5 x 3.8 cm

**gallop**

*FRONT TRACK LENGTH*

*FRONT TRACK WIDTH*

# Snowshoe Hare
*Lepus americanus*

Medium-size hare with long
ears and feet. Averages about
4 pounds (1.8 kg). Body
color is rusty to gray brown,
turning white in winter. Ears
retain their black tip in winter.

**Track:** Toes asymmetrical around
foot axis. Track indistinct because
the foot is completely haired and
lacks pads. Hind footprint may be up
to two and a half times longer than front.
To provide flotation on snow, hind feet
are exceptionally wide and toes may splay
apart so that width approaches length.

**Trail:** Hopping stride varies from 3–6 feet
(0.9–1.8 m). Tends to hop with paired
hind feet.

**Scat:** Dry scat is a slightly flattened
sphere. Produces a black, semiliquid
scat that is usually re-ingested to utilize
remaining nutrients.

**scat**
0.3 in.
0.8 cm

**chewed
branch
and cone**

SCAT WIDTH

**Habitat:** High mountains with deep snows. Dense second-growth forest is preferred, but swamps are also used. Forages at forest edge and in small clearings.

**Similar species:** Track differs from Eastern cottontail by its large, wide size.

**Other sign:** Look for woody plants—including conifers—that have had the tips of branches chewed off. During population highs, hares will strip tree bark and have been observed feeding on carcasses. The snowshoe's nest, a shallow depression known as a *form*, is found under conifer branches or logs.

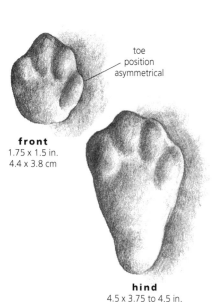

**front**
1.75 x 1.5 in.
4.4 x 3.8 cm

toe position asymmetrical

**hind**
4.5 x 3.75 to 4.5 in.
11.3 x 9.4 to 11.3 cm

**hop**

FRONT TRACK LENGTH

FRONT TRACK WIDTH

# Woodchuck
*Marmota monax*

**Size of a domestic cat, 5–10 pounds (2.2–4.5 kg). Ears and head are short and broad. Tail about one-third body length. Color frosted brown to yellowish brown on back, but paler on belly; dark feet.**

**Track:** Front foot size of a silver dollar, with four toes in 1-2-1 grouping. Five toes on hind foot in 1-3-1 grouping. Toes relatively slender. Four joined interdigital and two proximal pads on front footprint and four joined interdigital pads on hind foot. Heel is hairless.

**Trail:** A ground dweller, the woodchuck uses a half bound, which varies from 15 to 40 inches (33–88 cm). Walking stride is 18 inches (40 cm).

**Scat:** Rare to find because it is deposited in latrines within tunnel systems. Wide variety of forms, from oval pellets to long cords, all of which may be tightly stuck together. Sometimes lacks defined shape, being dark and runny when deposited.

**scat**
0.25–0.5 in.
0.6–1.3 cm

SCAT WIDTH

**Habitat:** Open or brushy areas, especially around rocky ravines and cultivated fields.

**Similar species:** Largest of the ground squirrels, its track dwarfs other ground squirrels. Track left when drinking at a stream may be distinguished from beaver's by lack of webbing and by having only four toes on front prints.

**Other sign:** Extensive tunnel system with two or more round-oval openings 5–7 inches (12.5–15 cm) in diameter. While some openings may have large mounds of dirt, others, excavated to the inside, may not have a mound and be more concealed. Fresh dirt indicates occupancy; if height of burrow opening exceeds 8 inches (18 cm), it may have been taken over by red fox.

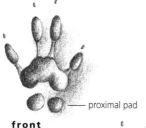

— proximal pad

**front**
2.2 x 1.8 in.
5.5 x 4.5 cm

**hind**
2.8 x 2 in.
7 x 5 cm

**bound**

FRONT TRACK LENGTH

FRONT TRACK WIDTH

# Thirteen-Lined Ground Squirrel

*Ictidomys (Spermophilus) tridecemlineatus*

Size of a small rat, 0.25–0.5 pound (113–227 g). Body is light to dark brown with thirteen white stripes or rows of spots. White belly.

**Track:** Front print has four toes, with 1-2-1 grouping. Hind has five toes, with 1-3-1 grouping. Toes relatively slender. Front footprint size of a quarter. Hind heel is hairless and may register clearly in track. Long claws may show, especially in front tracks.

**Trail:** Bounding stride averages 20 inches (44 cm). Uses a half bound, characteristic of its terrestrial lifestyle.

**Scat:** Small, usually unconnected, ovals.

**burrow entrance**

**scat**
0.1 in.
0.3 cm

SCAT WIDTH

**Habitat:** Found in grassy areas, including pastures and lawns of cemeteries and golf courses.

**Similar species:** Claws longer and feet smaller than those of tree squirrels. Smaller than woodchuck.

**Other sign:** Extensive burrow systems with a labyrinth of entranceways and galleries. Entrances are well hidden in vegetation and seldom have dirt at the openings.

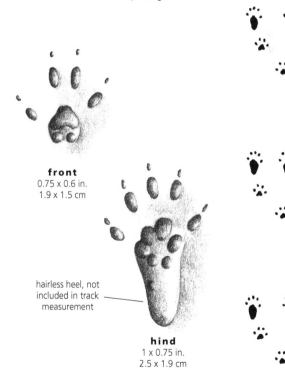

**front**
0.75 x 0.6 in.
1.9 x 1.5 cm

hairless heel, not
included in track
measurement

**hind**
1 x 0.75 in.
2.5 x 1.9 cm

**bound**

FRONT TRACK LENGTH

FRONT TRACK WIDTH

# Chipmunk
*Tamias* species

**Slightly larger than a large mouse, up to 3 ounces (80 g). Reddish fur, with white stripes bordered by black stripes along the sides of the face and body. Haired tail.**

**Track:** Front foot size of a nickel, with four toes in 1-2-1 grouping. Five toes on hind foot in 1-3-1 grouping. Toes relatively slender. Claws short. Hind heel is haired, and details are difficult to detect.

**Trail:** Bounding stride averages 7 inches (18 cm). Mostly terrestrial, it usually uses a half bound, though full bounds may be observed in its trails.

**Scat:** Small, usually unconnected, ovals.

**Habitat:** Deciduous forest and brush areas.

**scat**
0.1 in. diameter
0.3 cm

SCAT WIDTH

**Similar species:** Smaller than ground and tree squirrels. Lacks the long claws of ground squirrel. Smaller than woodchuck.

**Other sign:** Seeds and nuts of various plants, chewed open on one side.

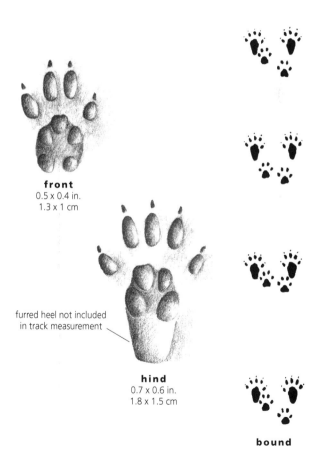

**front**
0.5 x 0.4 in.
1.3 x 1 cm

furred heel not included in track measurement

**hind**
0.7 x 0.6 in.
1.8 x 1.5 cm

**bound**

*FRONT TRACK LENGTH*

*FRONT TRACK WIDTH*

# Eastern Gray Squirrel
*Sciurus carolinensis*

**Large-size squirrel, weighing up to 1.5 pounds (0.7 kg). Grayish back with some brown in summer. Belly is whitish. Light colored ring around eye. Tail is bushy, bordered with white hairs**

**Track:** Front foot size of a half-dollar, with four toes in 1-2-1 grouping. Five toes on hind foot in 1-3-1 grouping. Toes relatively slender. Claws relatively short. Haired hind heel is indistinct in tracks.

**Trail:** Bounding stride ranges from 24–36 inches (60–90 cm). Straddle 5 inches (12.5 cm). Tends to use a full bound.

**Scat:** Small, shapeless black masses to small, usually unconnected, ovals.

**scat**
0.25 in.
0.6 cm

SCAT WIDTH

**Habitat:** Hardwood forests and river bottoms. Nut-producing trees in territory.

**Similar species:** Larger than chipmunk. Lacks the long claws of ground squirrels. Larger than red squirrel and smaller than woodchuck.

**Other sign:** Nests in tree holes and builds twig-and-leaf nests in branches of trees, about 25 feet (7.6 m) from the ground.

hind prints on front

**slow bound**

**front**
1.6 x 1 in.
4 x 2.5 cm

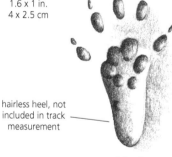

hairless heel, not included in track measurement

**hind**
2.6 x 1.4 in.
6.5 x 3.5 cm

**full bound**

*FRONT TRACK LENGTH*

*FRONT TRACK WIDTH*

# Red Squirrel
*Tamiasciurus hudsonicus*

Medium-size squirrel, weighing up to 0.5 pound (0.25 kg). Reddish brown back, separated from white underparts by a black stripe. White ring around eye. Slight ear tufts. Tail is bushy.

**Track:** Front foot size of a quarter, with four toes in 1-2-1 grouping and five pads. Five toes on hind foot in 1-3-1 grouping and four pads. Toes relatively slender. Claws relatively short. Haired hind heel is indistinct in tracks.

**Trail:** Full bounding stride averages 24 inches (60 cm). Walk and half bound when searching for food.

**Scat:** Small, shapeless black masses to small, usually unconnected, ovals.

**scat**
0.4 x 0.2 in.
1 x 0.5 cm

**chewed cones and seed casings**

*SCAT WIDTH*

**Habitat:** Boreal or northern coniferous forests, mixed hardwood forests, and swamps. Infrequently found in deciduous forests.

**Similar species:** Larger than chipmunk. Lacks the long claws of ground squirrel. Smaller than gray squirrel and woodchuck.

**Other sign:** Builds twig-and-leaf nests in branches of trees, about 15 feet (5 m) from the ground. Piles of pine and hemlock cone scales where squirrel removes scales to get at seeds. Cones are stored in a debris cache called a *midden* for use as winter food. Stripped buds of spruce trees scattered along forest floor.

hind
prints on
front

**slow bound**

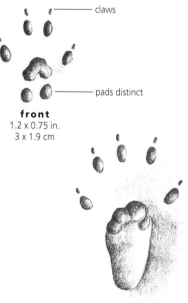

claws

pads distinct

**front**
1.2 x 0.75 in.
3 x 1.9 cm

**hind**
1.8 x 1 in.
4.5 x 2.5 cm

**full bound**

*FRONT TRACK LENGTH*

*FRONT TRACK WIDTH*

# Flying Squirrel—Northern and Southern

*Glaucomys sabrinus* and
*G. volans*

A small squirrel, weighing 4 ounces (112 g). Its silky fur is olive brown on the back and lead gray on the underside. A fold of skin stretches between front and hind legs and body, forming a "wing" and allowing the squirrel to glide. Its bushy tail is flattened to aid in sailing.

**Track:** Front foot size of a quarter, with four toes in 1-2-1 grouping. Five toes on hind foot in 1-3-1 grouping. Toes relatively slender. Claws relatively short and may not show. Hind foot interdigital pads form a tight crescent; proximal pads are lacking.

**Trail:** Bounding stride averages 20 inches (50 cm). Uses a full bound.

**scat**
0.1 in.
0.3 cm

SCAT WIDTH

**wing marks**

**Scat:** Small, usually unconnected, ovals.

**Habitat:** Deciduous and coniferous forests, though often found in attics of houses.

**Similar species:** Differs from all other squirrels and chipmunks by the tight crescent of interdigital pads on the hind foot. Lacks the long claws of ground squirrels. Smaller than woodchuck.

hind prints
on front

**Other sign:** More active at night. Skin flap outlines may show in dust or snow. Sometimes builds roof on bird's nest to use as den. Tree dens may hold twenty individuals during winter.

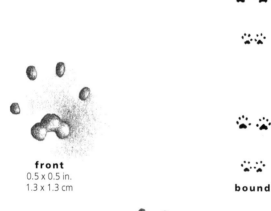

**front**
0.5 x 0.5 in.
1.3 x 1.3 cm

**bound**

interdigital pads
arrayed in a
crescent shape

**hind**
1.5 x 0.5 in.
3.8 x 1.3 cm

wing
drag

*FRONT TRACK LENGTH*

# Deer Mice
*Peromyscus maniculatus*

Small mice, weighing up to 1 ounce (28 g). Adults are reddish brown to brown on back with a white belly; juveniles are dark gray on the back with a light gray belly. Large eyes and ears. Tail is long and haired.

**Track:** Track smaller than a dime. Four toes on front foot in 1-2-1 grouping. Five toes on hind foot in 1-3-1 grouping. Four joined interdigital, one remnant, and two proximal pads on front footprint; five joined pads and heel on hind footprint. Heel is hairless.

**Trail:** Bounding stride averages 8 inches (20 cm). Those species that use a full bound are climbers and nest in grass, shrubs, or trees. Those species using a half bound nest on or below ground. Both types occasionally trot. Tail drag may be present.

**Scat:** Oval-shaped pellets similar to those left by house mice.

**scat**
0.1 in.
0.3 cm

SCAT WIDTH

**Habitat:** Ubiquitous, found from deserts to the northern tree line, from below sea level to the top of high peaks.

**Similar species:** Differ from shrew by having only four toes on the front feet and by being slightly larger. Differ from vole by often showing a tail drag and by most often bounding. Lack the long heel of the jumping mouse. Smaller than chipmunk.

**Other sign:** Compact grass nests without entrances may be found under logs, rocks, and boards. Enter and exit through the grass wall, which closes up after passage. Cache large quantities of seeds in any convenient protected area. Leave feces near and in nest.

**tail drag**

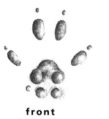
**front**
0.3 x 0.3 in.
0.8 x 0.8 cm

**4 x 4 bound**

**hind**
0.4 x 0.3 in.
1 x 0.8 cm

**3 x 3 bound**

*FRONT TRACK LENGTH*

*FRONT TRACK WIDTH*

# Voles
*Microtus* species

Many species of mouse-size mammals, related to lemmings and weighing up to 3 ounces (80 g). *Microtus* species, here represented by the meadow vole (*M. pennsylvanicus*), are gray to gray-brown on back, with a light-colored belly. Small, stocky mammals with short ears and small eyes, almost hidden by their fur. Short tails are sparsely haired.

**Track:** Track smaller than a dime. Four toes on front foot in 1-2-1 grouping. Five toes on hind foot in 1-3-1 grouping. Four joined interdigital and two proximal pads on front footprint and four interdigital pads and one proximal on hind footprint. Heel is hairless.

**Trail:** Trotting stride 6 inches (15 cm). Usually trot, seldom bound. Tails usually do not show in the trail.

**Scat:** Oval-shaped pellets similar to those left by house mice, often piled in tennis ball–size latrines that may hold hundreds of pellets.

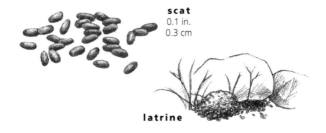

**scat**
0.1 in.
0.3 cm

**latrine**

*SCAT WIDTH*

**Habitat:** *Microtus* species are grass-loving species, found near meadows across North America and north to the Arctic.

**Similar species:** Differ from shrews by having only four toes on the front feet. Differ from mice by seldom showing a tail drag and by most often trotting. Lack the long heel of the jumping mouse.

**Other sign:** As snow melts in spring, grass nests lacking entrances may be found. Snow melt may also reveal 1-inch (2.5 cm) cords of grass and debris, stuffed into snow tunnels during winter to make space elsewhere in the tunnel network. Vole latrines are usually found near nests, while mice leave feces near and in their nests. Worn runways through the grass.

**bound**

**fast trot**

**trot**

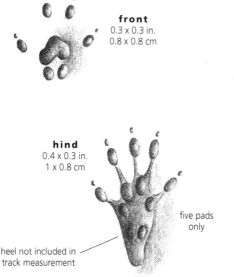

**front**
0.3 x 0.3 in.
0.8 x 0.8 cm

**hind**
0.4 x 0.3 in.
1 x 0.8 cm

five pads
only

heel not included in track measurement

FRONT TRACK LENGTH

FRONT TRACK WIDTH

# Meadow Jumping Mouse
*Zapus hudsonius*

A small, about 0.8 ounce (22 g), mouse with long hind feet and long, sparsely haired tail. Yellowish sides, darker brown back, and white belly. White tip on long tail.

**Track:** Four toes on front foot in 1-2-1 grouping. Hind foot is about the size of a quarter, exceptionally long and narrow, and has five toes in 1-3-1 grouping. Toes relatively slender. Heel is hairless.

**Trail:** Bounding stride 60–120 inches (150–300 cm). Makes sharp turns during travel. May cover considerable distance per stride when pursued. Tail drag often observed.

**scat**
0.1 in.
0.3 cm

SCAT WIDTH

**Scat:** Small oval pellets.

**Habitat:** Mountains, seldom found more than 3 feet (1 m) from a stream.

**Similar species:** Differs from other rodents in having long, narrow hind feet and tail drag. Differs from kangaroo rat by bounding from all four feet, not just hind.

**Other sign:** Small piles of grass stems left after eating. Round grass nests.

tail drag

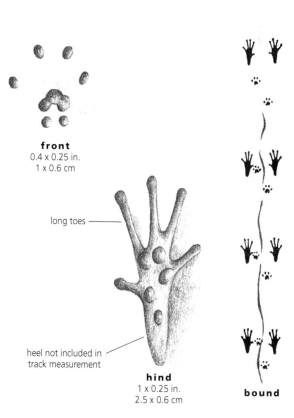

**front**
0.4 x 0.25 in.
1 x 0.6 cm

long toes

heel not included in
track measurement

**hind**
1 x 0.25 in.
2.5 x 0.6 cm

**bound**

FRONT TRACK LENGTH

FRONT TRACK WIDTH

# Plains Pocket Gopher
*Geomys bursarius*

Guinea pig–size rodent with minute eyes and ears and a short tail. External, fur-lined cheek pouches. Averages about 12 ounces (340 g), with males larger than females. Yellowish brown to dark, almost black. Two distinct grooves down front teeth.

**Track:** Five toes on both front and hind foot. Toes are relatively slender. Front feet have relatively long, wide claws for digging. Claw length is equal to or longer than toe length. Good tracks are seldom found, and more data is needed on track size. Measurements are approximate.

**Trail:** Walking stride is 6 inches (15 cm).

**Scat:** Thick, short cords.

**Habitat:** Needs deep sandy soils, preferably associated with grasslands, meadows, and fields.

**scat**
0.2 in.
0.5 cm

SCAT WIDTH

**Similar species:** Differs from other rodents by large, wide claws.

**Other sign:** Summer mounds consist of loose dirt forming a flat mound with no entrance visible (gophers close the tunnel as they go back underground). Winter casts of soil and rocks show where gophers packed dirt into snow tunnels while they burrowed for food. Scats are often found in the tunnel casts.

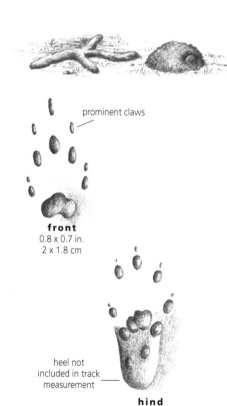

prominent claws

**front**
0.8 x 0.7 in.
2 x 1.8 cm

heel not included in track measurement

**hind**
1 x 0.7 in.
2.5 x 1.8 cm

**fast walk**

**walk**

FRONT TRACK LENGTH

FRONT TRACK WIDTH

# American Beaver
*Castor canadensis*

Largest rodent in North America, 30–60 pounds (14–27 kg). Distinguished by large, webbed hind feet and large, horizontally flattened tail. Fur overall is dark brown to almost black, with lighter belly.

**Track:** Front and hind prints show five toes. Hind foot may be larger than a human hand. Webbing between hind toes shows, but only when pulled tight by splaying of toes. Clear tracks are difficult to find, as the hind foot steps on the front foot and the dragging tail obliterates many prints.

**Trail:** Walking stride 18 inches (45 cm). Tail drag often visible.

**Scat:** Seldom found, as it is usually deposited in water, where it disintegrates quickly. Marshmallow-size, a little longer than thick. Consist of wood chips.

**Habitat:** Seldom found far from a creek, river, pond, or lake.

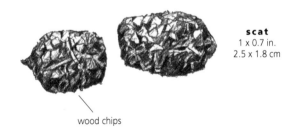

**scat**
1 x 0.7 in.
2.5 x 1.8 cm

wood chips

SCAT WIDTH

**Similar species:** Differs from other rodents by large size and webbing. Differs from river otter by long, slender toes and pointed heel, and by lacking a chevron-shaped pad.

**Other sign:** Dams and conical lodges built of twigs and sticks. Standing, cut-off tree trunks end in a tapered cone. Debarked tree limbs in the water.

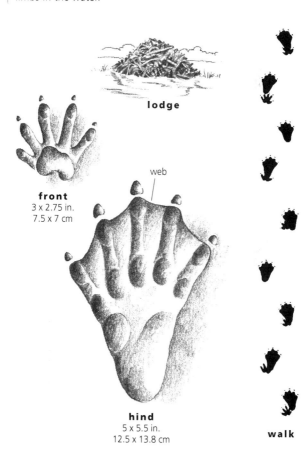

**lodge**

**front**
3 x 2.75 in.
7.5 x 7 cm

web

**hind**
5 x 5.5 in.
12.5 x 13.8 cm

**walk**

*FRONT TRACK LENGTH*

*FRONT TRACK WIDTH*

# Muskrat
*Ondatra zibethica*

Large, rat-like, stocky, up to 4 pounds (2 kg). Males slightly larger than females. Small eyes and ears. Tail is black, flattened, scaly, with few hairs.

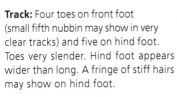

**Track:** Four toes on front foot (small fifth nubbin may show in very clear tracks) and five on hind foot. Toes very slender. Hind foot appears wider than long. A fringe of stiff hairs may show on hind foot.

**Trail:** Walking strides averages 11 inches (28 cm). May lope with body turned to side. Tail drag often visible.

**Scat:** Oval, at most three to four times longer than wide. Often deposited in a sticky mass on exposed logs at water's edge.

**Habitat:** Marshes and lake edges, secondarily on streambanks. Large rivers are not as frequently used. Cattails and rushes predominate.

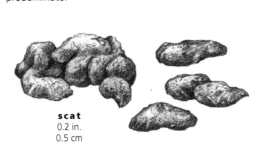

**scat**
0.2 in.
0.5 cm

SCAT WIDTH

**Similar species:** Differs from beaver by smaller size and lack of webbing. Differs from mink by long slender toes and by usually walking.

**Other sign:** Small conical domes made from reeds serve as dens. Cut grass and reeds near water's edge mark feeding sites. Muskrats make "post offices," repeated scat deposits, on rocks.

**4 x 4 bound**

**3 x 3 bound**

**post office**

**side lope**

**front**
1.3 x 1.2 in.
3.3 x 3 cm

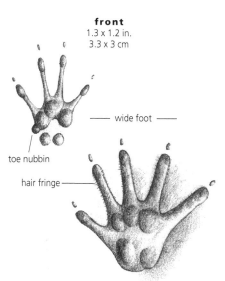

— wide foot —

toe nubbin

hair fringe

**fast walk**

**hind**
1.3 x 1.6 in.
3.3 x 4 cm

**walk**

FRONT TRACK LENGTH

FRONT TRACK WIDTH

# Porcupine
*Erethizon dorsatum*

Basketball-size or larger, 10–25 pounds (5–11 kg). Stocky body, with short legs. Distinguished by the presence of quills. Brown to yellowish brown in color.

**Track:** Rough texture formed by small nubs on soles of feet. Four toes on front foot and five toes on hind. Toes often do not show. Claws often show, especially on front tracks.

**Trail:** Walking stride 17 inches (43 cm). Tail drag often present.

**Scat:** Winter scat formed from feeding on conifers is red. Summer scat includes more herbs and shrubs and is brown to

**scat**
0.5 in.
1.3 cm

**debarked stick with chew marks**

black. Scat from both seasons may be composed of individual pellets or strings of pellets connected by fibers.

**Habitat:** Generally found near forests, but may be far from trees if shrubs are available.

**Similar species:** Rough texture on sole of foot is diagnostic. In snow, trough made by dragging belly highlights its stockiness, separating it from faster-moving mammals.

**Other sign:** Twigs with bark chewed off, found at the bases of trees. Porcupines will perch in a tree for days, chewing the bark, thereby killing the tree.

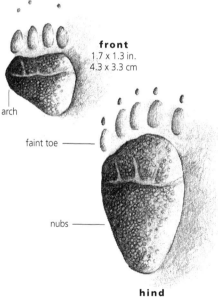

front
1.7 x 1.3 in.
4.3 x 3.3 cm

arch

faint toe

nubs

hind
2.7 x 1.7 in.
6.8 x 4.3 cm

tail
drag

**amble**

**walk**

FRONT TRACK LENGTH

FRONT TRACK WIDTH

# Moose
*Alces alces*

Largest member of deer family. Considerable regional variation exists, but male may weigh 900 pounds (400 kg), with female smaller. Color varies from tan to blackish. Females have a white patch of hair around the vulva (visible at a distance) that helps identify sex. Male has antlers that are shed annually.

**Track:** Long, with the pad extending to near the front of the hoof. Subunguis region is narrow. Track is delicate for the weight of the animal.

**Trail:** Walking stride is 70 inches (175 cm). Seldom gallops. Trots when in a hurry.

**Scat:** Most of the year consists of dry pellets that scatter on impact with the ground. When the diet is moist, nipple-dimple shape predominates. Winter scat is oval and consists mostly of chips of woody vegetation.

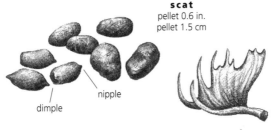

**scat**
pellet 0.6 in.
pellet 1.5 cm

nipple

dimple

**antler**

SCAT WIDTH

**Habitat:** Mixed conifer and hardwood forests containing willows and aspen or poplar. Streams and shallow lakes provide aquatic vegetation.

**Similar species:** Differs from elk in that the pad occupies most of each clout. Differs from deer by being larger and more pointed, with larger subunguis.

**Other sign:** In removing velvet from their antlers, bulls strip bark from young saplings and break off limbs, often killing the trees. Height of tree wound shows animal height.

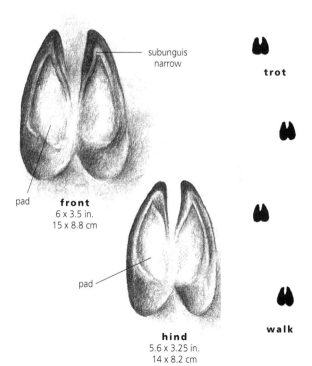

subunguis narrow

**trot**

pad

**front**
6 x 3.5 in.
15 x 8.8 cm

pad

**walk**

**hind**
5.6 x 3.25 in.
14 x 8.2 cm

FRONT TRACK LENGTH

FRONT TRACK WIDTH

# White-tailed Deer
*Odocoileus virginianus*

Smallest member of the deer family. Male averages 130 pounds (60 kg), female about 110 pounds (50 kg). Coat is reddish in summer and blue-gray in winter. The prominent white tail is carried erect when animal is disturbed. Antlers, found only on male, have tines, or points, branching off main beam.

**Track:** Heart shaped, with convex wall. Pad occupies most of the clout; subunguis slender.

**Trail:** Walking stride 30 inches (75 cm). Pronks or stots with front and hind feet striking the ground at the same time. Gallops when in a hurry.

**Scat:** Usually dry, falls apart when it hits the ground. Pellets vary from nipple-dimple shape to oval.

**scat**
pellet 0.3 in.
pellet 0.8 cm

**antler**

SCAT WIDTH

**Habitat:** Generally closed timber, but moves out to grasslands at twilight to feed.

**Similar species:** Smaller than elk; has more slender tips, and pad occupies most of clout.

**Other sign:** Gathers ("yards" up) in large numbers in sheltered groves during winter. Breaks off limbs of trees when removing velvet from antlers. Velvet is difficult to find, as both deer and rodents eat the nutrient-rich material. Height of tree wound indicates animal height.

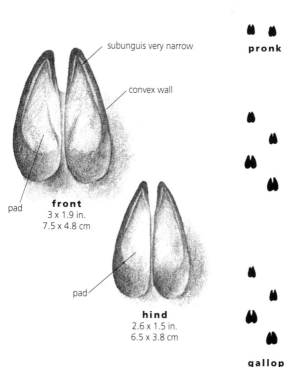

subunguis very narrow

convex wall

**front**
3 x 1.9 in.
7.5 x 4.8 cm

pad

pad

**hind**
2.6 x 1.5 in.
6.5 x 3.8 cm

**pronk**

**gallop**

FRONT TRACK LENGTH

FRONT TRACK WIDTH

# Elk
*Cervus (elaphus) canadensis*

Medium-size, larger than deer, males averaging 700 pounds (315 kg) and females 450 pounds (200 kg). Reddish to dark brown, with a yellow rump patch. Males shed antlers annually. Also known as wapiti. Reintroduced in the Great Lakes region.

**Track:** Blocky, with each clout wide at the leading tip. Pad of hoof occupies rear quarter of each clout; subunguis occupies remaining three-quarters of each clout.

**Trail:** Walking stride 52 inches (130 cm). When chased by a predator, gallops and occasionally pronks.

**Scat:** Most of the year, scat consists of pellets that scatter on impact with the ground. When the diet is moist, nipple-dimple shape predominates, changing to oval as vegetation dries. When scat is moist, pellets stick together.

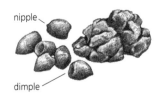

nipple

dimple

**scat**
pellet 0.5 in.
pellet 1.3 cm

**antler**

SCAT WIDTH

**Habitat:** Forest. Beds in dense trees during the day, moving out into clearings to graze during twilight hours.

**Similar species:** Differs from deer and moose by having a small pad at the rear of the hoof.

**Other sign:** Removing antler velvet, bulls strip bark from young saplings and break off limbs, often killing the trees. Height of tree wound shows animal height. Bulls make mud wallows in the fall. During rut, look for areas where bulls have sparred with the ground using their antlers.

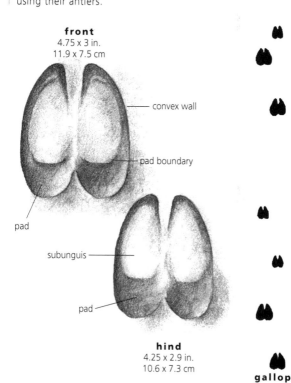

**front**
4.75 x 3 in.
11.9 x 7.5 cm

— convex wall

— pad boundary

pad

subunguis —

pad —

**hind**
4.25 x 2.9 in.
10.6 x 7.3 cm

**pronk**

**gallop**

*FRONT TRACK LENGTH*

*FRONT TRACK WIDTH*

# Selected Reading

### Tracks and Tracking

Bang, P., et al. 1972. *Collins Guide to Animal Tracks and Signs.* London: Collins Sons.

Brown, R., J. Ferguson, M. Lawrence, and D. Lees. 1987. *Tracks and Signs of the Birds of Britain and Europe: An Identification Guide.* Kent, England: Christopher Helm.

Brunner, J. 1909. *Tracks and Tracking.* New York: Outing.

Elbroch, M. 2003. *Mammal Tracks and Signs: A Guide to North American Species.* Mechanicsburg, PA: Stackpole Books.

Elbroch, M., and E. Marks. 2001. *Bird Tracks and Signs: A Guide to North American Species.* Mechanicsburg, PA: Stackpole Books.

Elbroch, M., L. Liebenberg, and A. Louw. 2010. *Practical Tracking: A Guide to Following Footprints and Finding Animals.* Mechanicsburg, PA: Stackpole Books.

Fjelline, D. P., and T. M. Mansfield. 1989. "Method to Standardize the Procedure for Measuring Mountain Lion Tracks." In *Proceedings of the Third Mountain Lion Workshop,* ed. R. H. Smith, 49–51. Prescott, AZ: Arizona Game and Fish Department.

Forrest, L. R. 1988. *Field Guide to Tracking Animals in Snow.* Harrisburg, PA: Stackpole Books.

Halfpenny, J. C. 1997. *Tracking: Mastering the Basics.* A Naturalist's World. DVD.

Halfpenny, J. C., et al. 2009. *Track Plates for Mammals.* Gardiner, MT: A Naturalist's World.

Halfpenny, J. C., and T. D. Furman. 2010. *Tracking Wolves: The Basics.* Gardiner, MT: A Naturalist's World.

Halfpenny, J. C., et al. 1996. "Snow Tracking." In *American Marten, Fisher, Lynx, and Wolverines: Survey Methods for Their Detection,* ed. W. Zielinski and T. Kucera, 91–163. General Technical Report PSW-GTR-157. Berkeley, CA: USDA Forest Service, Pacific Southwest Research Station.

———. 1986a. *A Field Guide to Mammal Tracking in North America.* Boulder, CO: Johnson.

———. 1986b. *Tracks and Tracking: A "How To" Guide.* Gardiner, MT: A Naturalist's World. DVD.

Headstrom, R. 1971. *Identifying Animals Tracks: Mammals, Birds, and Other Animals of the Eastern United States.* New York: Dover.

Liebenberg, L. 2010. *Practical Tracking: A Guide to Following Footprints and Finding Animals.* Mechanicsburg, PA: Stackpole Books.

Lowery, J. C. 2006. *The Tracker's Field Guide.* Guilford, CT: FalconGuides.

Moskowitz, D. 2010. *Wildlife of the Pacific Northwest: Tracking and Identifying Mammals, Birds, Reptiles, Amphibians, and Invertebrates.* Portland, OR: Timber Press.

Murie, O. 1954. *A Field Guide to Animal Tracks.* Peterson Field Guide Series, no. 9. Boston: Houghton Mifflin.

Rezendes, P. 1999. *Tracking and the Art of Seeing: How to Read Animal Tracks and Signs.* 2nd ed. Charlotte, VT: Camden House.

Seton, E. T. 1958. *Animal Tracks and Hunter Signs.* New York: Doubleday.

## Recommended Field Identification Guides

Burt, W. H., and R. P. Grossenheider. 1964. *A Field Guide to the Mammals.* Peterson Field Guide Series, no. 5. Boston: Houghton Mifflin.

Chandlers, S. R., B. Bruun, and H. S. Zim. 1983. *A Guide to Field Identification: Birds of North America.* New York: Golden.

Conant, R. 1958. *Reptiles and Amphibians of Eastern and Central North America.* Peterson Field Guide Series, no. 12. Boston: Houghton Mifflin.

Dunn, J. L., and J. Alderfer. 1983. *Field Guide to the Birds of North America.* Washington, DC: National Geographic Society.

Gosner, K. L. 1985. *Atlantic Seashore.* Norwalk, CT: The Easton Press.

Kays, R. W., and D. E. Wilson. 2002. *Mammals of North America.* Princeton, NJ: Princeton University Press.

Peterson, R. T. 1984. *Birds of the Eastern United States.* Norwalk, CT: The Easton Press.

# Index

## About the Author

**James Halfpenny** is president of both A Naturalist's World and Track Scene Investigation (forensic track investigation). Annually Jim teaches programs across North America and leads Arctic expeditions for the aurora borealis, polar bears, and polar ice.

Jim has searched for dinosaur tracks in Colorado and Montana, tracked wildlife in Tanzania and Kenya, studied endangered species on China's Tibet-Qinghai Plateau, and researched the polar bears of Hudson Bay and Greenland. Since 1961 he has taught outdoor and environmental education for a vast array of schools and organizations, including the Appalachian Mountain Club, Defenders of Wildlife, National Audubon Society, National Outdoor Leadership School, National Wildlife Federation, Outward Bound, Smithsonian Institution, Teton Science School, Wilderness Society, and Yellowstone Association Institute. He has trained rangers in tracking techniques at Yellowstone, Glacier, Grand Teton, and Rocky Mountain National Parks and personnel from many state departments of natural resources. His research has also taken him to all seven continents including Antarctica and all over North America. Jim has been featured with Australian aborigines, Kalahari bushmen, and Alaskan Inuit in a documentary about the loss of native tracking skills shown on the Discovery Channel and debunking Bigfoot tracks on *Monster Quest*.

Jim is author of the laminated field guide series Tracks, Scats and Signs. He is also the senior author of the Scats and Tracks series, *A Field Guide to Mammal Tracking in North America*, *Track Plates for Mammals*, *Tracking Wolves: The Basics*, *Yellowstone Bears in the Wild*, *Yellowstone Wolves in the Wild*, *Charting Yellowstone Wolves*, *Discovering Yellowstone Wolves: Watcher's Guide*, and *Winter: An Ecological Handbook*.

Jim is a past field director and research associate for the University of Colorado's Institute of Arctic and Alpine Research. He is a fellow of the Explorer's Club and a Vietnam War veteran. He lives just outside Yellowstone National Park in Gardiner, Montana.

## About the Illustrator

**Todd Telander** is an artist and naturalist living in Walla Walla, Washington. He has illustrated several books in the FalconGuides series in addition to providing artwork for clients nationwide, including the Denver Museum of Natural History, the Maui Ocean Center, and the American Birding Association. Currently he paints landscapes and wildlife, teaches art classes, and operates the Telander Gallery with his wife, Kirsten, a writer.